1.
PHOTO ©CHRIS E. HEISEY/PLACE STOCK PHOTO.COM

2.
PHOTO ©JEFF D. NICHOLAS

3.
PHOTO ©JAMES P. ROWAN

4.
PHOTO ©JEFF D. NICHOLAS

5.
PHOTO ©JEFF D. NICHOLAS

1: John Brown's Fort, Harpers Ferry, WV. **2:** Artillery and the Henry House, Henry Hill, Manassas, MD. **3:** The Stone (or Matthew) House, Manassas, MD. **4:** Detail of an Ohio infantry monument, Chickamauga Battlefield, GA. **5:** The McLean House, Appomattox Court House, VA.

CIVIL
WAR
BATTLEFIELDS

THE
LANDSCAPES OF WAR

BY

SCOTT THYBONY

SIERRA PRESS
MARIPOSA, CA

ACKNOWLEDGMENTS

No book of this sort could exist without the dedicated efforts of the National Park Service to preserve these places of war and pass on the legacy of courage and sacrifice they represent. To the park historians and interpreters who assisted my efforts, you have my appreciation. And to my friend Ed Bearss I owe a debt of gratitude for his encouragement and enthusiasm. As the two of us tromped over the old battlefields, pushing from dawn to late in the evening, his recounting of events in hypnotic detail evoked a tangible sense of what those soldiers had experienced. Strangers, drawn by his commanding voice, would gather close to listen, and I soon stopped asking questions and let the cadence of his narration stir the past.   —S.T.

FRONT COVER
11th Pennsylvania Monument on Oak Ridge, Gettysburg, PA. PHOTO ©CHRIS E. HEISEY/PLACE STOCK PHOTO.COM

INSIDE FRONT COVER
Antietam Creek and Lower (or Burnside) Bridge, Antietam, MD. PHOTO ©TERRY DONNELLY

PAGE 2
New York Artillery Monument and dogwoods, Devils Den, Gettysburg, PA. PHOTO ©TERRY DONNELLY

TITLE PAGE
Bugler detail on the Virginia Memorial, Seminary Ridge, Gettysburg, PA. PHOTO ©CHRIS E. HEISEY/PLACE STOCK PHOTO.COM

OPPOSITE
Confederate artillery on Seminary Ridge, Gettysburg, PA. PHOTO ©TERRY DONNELLY

PAGE 4 (BELOW)
Union artillery on Stevens Knoll, Gettysburg, PA. PHOTO ©CHRIS E. HEISEY/PLACE STOCK PHOTO.COM

PAGE 6/7
The Stone House, used as a field hospital during both battles at Manassas (Bull Run), VA. PHOTO ©CHARLES GURCHE

PAGE 7 (LOWER RIGHT)
Wisconsin Infantry Monument, Chickamauga, GA. PHOTO ©JEFF D. NICHOLAS

CONTENTS

THE AMERICAN BATTLEFIELD

A dead calm hangs over the battlefield of Antietam as the two of us reach the top of a rise above an old farm road. Union soldiers charged up this slope long ago and half of them never marched back down. Historian Ed Bearss and I are walking the ground to place those distant events in the terrain where they occurred, tracing on foot the rolling fields that funneled so many men to their deaths.

We have approached this spot from a direction few take, climbing a slope where the grass grows thick and untrammeled. Bearss has led me along the route taken by a Union brigade as it attacked the Confederates waiting in a sunken road now known as Bloody Lane. We find ourselves silhouetted against the sky within killing range of the enemy lines, and the tension builds. It is September 17, 1862.

"You're now under fire," says Bearss. "You're under fire from the artillery and you're under fire from the infantry, but you're still advancing." As we close the distance, he relates the story of the Irish Brigade, its aspirations and its failed dreams, the golden harp on its emerald flag, and the Gaelic war cry of its men. "Now we halt here," he continues, "and for the next thirty minutes, at a range of less than fifty yards, the Irish Brigade and the Confederates posted in the sunken road will blaze away at each other."

As he talks, terrifying images fill the scene before us. Cries of the living and dying cut through the roar of battle as the air pulses with concussive waves of cannon fire and each blade of grass shakes with the impact of bullets. "Finally," he says, "the Irish pull back; they've had it."

Before the day ends, the sunken road will fill with bodies as tightly packed as a river jammed with logs. The fighting in this sector alone will result in a combined loss of 5,000 soldiers killed, wounded, and captured. Four times that number will appear on the list of total casualties, when the battle ceases and the bloodiest day in American history ends.

Greatly outnumbering the armies of those days, visitors throng to the battlefield parks each year to connect with the past. Bearss, former chief historian of the National Park Service, has guided thousands across these landscapes and knows the impact the experience can have. Reactions range from anger to awe, and sometimes the tears flow freely. "It brings out the emotions," he says. And emotions often run as high about protecting the battle sites as they do about the war itself.

The idea of preserving battlefields began while the war still raged. Many of those at the Battle of Gettysburg, for example, realized its significance as they fought it. A few months later, in a famous address that every schoolchild can recite, U.S.

TOP: Confederate fatalities at Sunken Road (Bloody Lane), Antietam, MD, 1862. **MIDDLE:** President-elect Abraham Lincoln as he appeared prior to taking office, 1859—compare this photograph with the portrait of Lincoln on page 55 that was taken at the conclusion of the Civil War. **BOTTOM:** Confederate casualties along Hagerstown Pike, Antietam, MD, 1862.
PHOTOS COURTESY LIBRARY of CONGRESS

OPPOSITE: Sculpture of Union Commander, General George Gordon Meade, Cemetery Ridge, Gettysburg, PA. PHOTO ©LARRY ULRICH

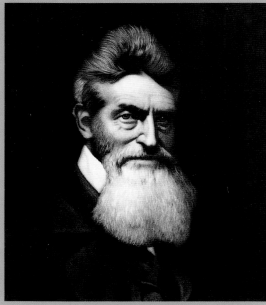

TOP: Destroyed railroad bridge at the confluence of the Shenandoah and Potomac Rivers, Harpers Ferry, WV, 1862. **MIDDLE:** Five generations of a slave family at Smith's Plantation, Beaufort, SC, 1862. **BOTTOM:** Portrait of abolitionist John Brown.
PHOTOS COURTESY LIBRARY of CONGRESS

President Abraham Lincoln articulated how the struggle and sacrifice of the soldiers had turned a swath of Pennsylvania farmlands into hallowed ground. His words set the stage for those who took steps to transform the landscape of war into a place to honor the dead and inspire the living.

Years after the war, Congress began by selecting several decisive battles out of seventy-six major engagements and thousands of lesser ones. Chickamauga and Chattanooga became the first battlefield park, followed by Antietam, Shiloh, Gettysburg, and Vicksburg. Today, the National Park Service runs dozens of Federally preserved historical sites, military parks, monuments, and national battlefields from the Civil War period. Among these are Fort Sumter, which received the first shot of the conflict, and Harpers Ferry, where a raid by northern abolitionists set the stage for the nation-shaping events to come.

On December 2, 1859, abolitionist John Brown climbed the thirteen steps of the gallows only weeks after launching an attack on the federal armory and arsenal at Harpers Ferry. His plan to inspire a slave uprising had failed, but he would achieve his ultimate goal. His raid galvanized the North and confirmed the worst fears of the South, as a nation divided in spirit headed toward open hostilities.

Differences between the manufacturing regions of the North and the agricultural South had steadily grown into bitter disagreements. The economic disparity was obvious. Northern factories produced 90 percent of the nation's industrial goods, with New York alone manufacturing twice as much as the southern states combined. Southern traditions were deeply rooted in the land itself, whether through small family farms or large cotton and sugar plantations worked by slaves. For years political leaders had maneuvered to reach compromises, buying time but ultimately resolving nothing. Fundamental differences between the slaveholding states and the northern regions grew increasingly confrontational when efforts failed to reconcile the issue of slavery with America's founding vision of freedom and equality.

Southerners saw the election of Abraham Lincoln less than a year after John Brown's execution as proof the radical abolitionists had seized the reins of government. They bitterly opposed his stand on the gradual emancipation of slaves. The southern states believed they had the right to withdraw their consent to be governed by an association of states now working against their interests. They valued loyalty to the home state over duty to the Union and would fight if an army invaded their native soil. Those in the North, more comfortable with the growing powers of a central government, gave their allegiance to an undivided nation and would go to war to prevent the country from being split down the middle.

With Lincoln's election, South Carolina seceded from the Union and other southern states quickly followed. Cannons of the newly formed Confederate States soon bombarded the federal garrison at Fort Sumter when it refused to either evacuate or surrender. Lincoln reacted to the firing on the United States flag with a call for 75,000 militiamen to defeat those states in open rebellion. War fever swept the nation, with both sides confident of a quick victory. The *New York Times* predicted it would end within a month; few thought it would take four years and cost the lives of more than 620,000 soldiers and uncounted thousands of civilians. And few could guess the events now set in motion would end with the Union intact and America unshackled from slavery.

Harpers Ferry, West Virginia and the confluence of the Shenandoah (left) and Potomac (center) Rivers seen from Maryland Heights, Maryland. PHOTO ©CHRIS E. HEISEY/PLACE STOCK PHOTO.COM

Harpers Ferry lies at the dramatic confluence of the Potomac and Shenandoah Rivers, enclosed by commanding heights. The federal government built an armory here in 1799, and the industrial town grew into a bustling transportation hub.

On the night of October 16, 1859, John Brown led twenty-one men in an attack on the government arsenal. He intended to capture enough of the 100,000 muskets stored there to equip an army of liberation and take the fight against slavery to the South. This new, more volatile phase of the conflict pushed the nation closer to war.

Not a single slave willingly joined his short-lived raid, which ended less than two days later when federal troops killed or captured Brown and his followers. On the day of his execution, the abolitionist handed a note to his jailer containing a dark warning.

"I, John Brown," he wrote, "am now quite certain that the crimes of this guilty land will never be purged away, but with Blood. I had, as I now think, vainly flattered myself that without very much bloodshed, it might be done."

A man who would do his part to fulfill this prophesy stood in the ranks of militiamen as the noose was placed around Brown's neck. Few civilians were allowed to attend the execution, so John Wilkes Booth had finessed his way into the elite Richmond Grays, sharing their militia duty and reciting Shakespeare around the campfire at night. "I helped to hang John Brown," he wrote after witnessing the hanging, "and while I live, I shall think with joy upon the day when I saw the sun go down upon one traitor *less* within our land."

Across the North, church bells tolled when word of the abolitionist's death reached the region. "Even now as I write," commented author Henry Wadsworth Longfellow, "they are leading old John Brown to execution in Virginia for attempting to rescue slaves! This is sowing the wind to reap the whirlwind, which will come soon."

The pace of events quickened. The day after Virginia seceded, federal soldiers guarding the U.S. Armory and Arsenal set fire to the buildings, burning the arsenal and its store of arms. But the armory survived, and southern soldiers soon seized the machinery so crucial for the war effort. Strategically located, Harpers Ferry changed hands eight times during the four years of fighting. In the run-up to the battle of Antietam, Stonewall Jackson captured the town's garrison of 12,500 men, the largest surrender of Union troops during the war. After the fighting ended, Harpers Ferry, the setting for John Brown's strike against slavery, continued to serve as a symbol of freedom as the nation rebuilt.

1861: THE FATE OF A NATION

A single week in the spring of 1861 sealed the fate of a nation. During the early months of the year, nothing was certain; war might still be averted. Seven southern states had voted to secede but others still opposed the creation of a separate country. In his inaugural speech, the new President, Abraham Lincoln, pledged not to be the first to use force, leaving the door open to reconciliation. But the country had reached a breaking point.

At dawn on April 12, events suddenly cascaded into open war. The Confederate batteries surrounding Charleston Harbor, South Carolina opened fire on Fort Sumter. When news of the bombardment flashed across the country, all the uncertainties and bitterness of the preceding years erupted in wildly cheering crowds throughout the South and patriotic enthusiasm in the North. "The firing on Fort Sumter," wrote Virginian Luther Hopkins, "was like throwing a stone into a hornet's nest."

A terrific cannonade pounded the United States fort, and on April 13 Major Robert Anderson ordered his men to lower the Stars and Stripes. Fort Sumter had become a symbol of United States sovereignty, and firing on the American flag was an act of war. Two days later, Lincoln called on the loyal states to provide the federal army with 75,000 militia to suppress the rebellion. Few could then imagine that army would grow to a million men by the war's end.

For Virginia to comply with Lincoln's order meant taking up arms against states that shared its southern traditions. Instead, on April 17, it voted to secede. Three states followed, bringing the number of breakaway Southern states to eleven, with a combined population of more than nine million—a third of those slaves. The North retained twenty-three states and seven territories, with a population of twenty-two million. The South faced long odds, and before the fighting ended, one out of every four men of military age would die. On April 19, a week after hostilities began, Lincoln ordered a blockade of much of the southern coast on the same day troops came under attack in the streets of Baltimore.

Massachusetts had responded quickly to Lincoln's call for soldiers, sending several militia regiment to reinforce the nation's capital. At Baltimore, troops of the 4th Massachusetts began transferring between rail stations in horse-drawn cars. An angry mob barricaded the streets and attacked them, forcing several companies to continue on foot. The troops started taking casualties as the crowd pelted them with stones and dragged a few off to be beaten. As the mob pressed in, the violence escalated. Officers gave the order to fire, and when it was over four soldiers and

TOP: Fort Sumter (in distance) seen from Confederate Fort Johnson, Charleston, SC. **MIDDLE:** The battered walls of Fort Sumter, Charleston, SC. **BOTTOM:** Union Major Robert Anderson.
PHOTOS COURTESY LIBRARY of CONGRESS

OPPOSITE: Statue of Confederate General Thomas "Stonewall" Jackson on Henry Hill, Manassas, VA. PHOTO ©CHRIS E. HEISEY/PLACE STOCK PHOTO.COM

TOP: Escaped slaves, or "contrabands", at Cumberland Landing, VA. **MIDDLE:** Building that once housed slave pens, Alexandria, VA. **BOTTOM:** "Auction & Negro Sales" office, Atlanta, GA.
PHOTOS COURTESY LIBRARY of CONGRESS

twelve civilians lay dead. For the duration of the war, Baltimore would remain under Union control.

States, north and south, began frantic efforts to raise troops for the coming fight, which most thought would end in a single, decisive battle. Opinion makers on both sides believed the issue could be resolved with a minimum loss of life. At the end of May the Confederate capital moved to Richmond, Virginia, and the hundred miles separating the opposing capitals would soon become the war's most contested battleground.

The South, with limited resources, chose a strategy that focused its efforts on the eastern theater of operations, often neglecting the central and western theaters, where armies would grapple for control of the Mississippi. It chose to wage a defensive war, gaining the advantage of shorter supply lines and a loyal populace, while casting the Union forces as aggressors. Realizing a long war of attrition would lead to defeat, they pinned their hopes on winning diplomatic recognition from the key European powers.

Men on both sides of the conflict saw themselves as patriots. Southerners fought a war to preserve the form of government, with its tolerance of slavery, established by the American Revolution of 1776. Northern soldiers marched off to battle with a desire to preserve the constitutionally established union of states. Only later in the conflict did ending slavery become a political goal of the North.

But whatever the stated reasons for going to war, slavery remained the emotional force driving it. In the first year, long before emancipation was proclaimed, the slaves began escaping to the Union lines, where the northerners came face to face with the realities of slavery. A Union army chaplain, deeply affected by a slave he met in occupied territory, recorded the story of Hanson, born into slavery in Alexandria, Virginia. When his master broke a promise to set him free, Hanson began planning his escape. For years he studied the routes leading north and saved what little money he could earn. His only chance of success was to keep the plan absolutely secret, so he told no one, not even his wife and children. Their fate would depend on his ability to earn enough to purchase their freedom once he escaped. When the time came, the slave crossed the Potomac River and at night slipped through Washington, DC. With his life-long dream of freedom lying wide open before him, he hesitated, unable to shake the memory of those he had left behind.

"I could not see my way," Hanson said; "my tears blinded my eyes. I felt their arms around my neck, and their soft faces on my cheek, and their little hands were pressing me back. I wandered, not knowing where I was going, until I found myself standing on the bank of the Potomac, looking over at my cabin." His desire for freedom had been so overwhelming he thought nothing could stand in his way, but before morning, Hanson recrossed the river and returned home. "Nature was too strong for me," he said. ". . . I never tried again."

With war at hand, the public wanted a quick resolution to the conflict. Southern newspapers pressured their new government to strike Washington, while headlines in northern newspapers demanded, "Forward to Richmond!" Thousands of raw recruits poured into camps in the nation's capital, while the Confederate troops gathered thirty miles west near Manassas, Virginia.

In the heat of July, the Union army lumbered into Virginia as the Confederates took up positions behind Bull Run and waited for an attack. When it came, they were taken by surprise. The northern army turned their flank and began driving them from the field. At the crux of the battle, Confederate general Thomas "Stonewall" Jackson rallied the retreating Southerners and hit back with a strong counterpunch. As Confederate reinforcements poured onto the field, the Union army collapsed in a headlong retreat back to Washington.

The Union rout at Manassas shocked the North, and by forgetting how close they came to losing the battle, it reaffirmed the South's confidence in its military superiority. That fall, a probe across the Potomac at Ball's Bluff ended in another northern defeat. But under the leadership of George McClellan, the Union army began to remake itself, responding to its losses with renewed determination. For the remainder of the year both sides struggled to raise and train their armies, knowing the real contest lay ahead.

With attention focused on the east, events critical to the outcome of the war were occurring farther west. The North began implementing an effective strategy to keep the border states of Missouri, Kentucky, and Maryland from joining the Confederacy. To this end, Lincoln downplayed the antislavery issue and used every tool available, including military occupation and the suspension of civil liberties, to prevent those states from bolting. He went so far as to imprison, without trial, thirty-one Maryland legislators who were preparing to vote for secession.

In August, the Confederates won a victory at Wilson's Creek in Missouri, which they followed up by forcing the surrender of a Union garrison at Lexington. Unable to consolidate these victories, the southern forces eventually withdrew to a corner of the state. Kentucky tried to maintain its neutrality, but went with the North after a southern army was the first to cross its borders. Northern forces under McClellan entered the pro-Union section of northwest Virginia to secure the Baltimore and Ohio Railroad, a strategically important link between east and west. Torn apart by divided loyalties, the border states suffered from a vicious guerilla war and became, in Lincoln's words, "a killing field."

Fort Sumter fell to the Confederacy, but Forts Pickens and Taylor in Florida and Fort Monroe commanding Virginia's Hampton Roads remained in federal hands. These footholds aided efforts to blockade the southern coast, a crucial element of Lincoln's strategy. Using the North's overwhelming naval superiority, he placed an economic stranglehold on the rebellious states. Union amphibious forces also bombarded and seized key points on the coast of the Carolinas to supply Naval operations. These efforts grew more efficient with each passing month, as the navy cut off the export of cotton and hampered the import of crucial war material.

The year 1861 saw the nation fractured by war. Life-and-death struggles had shaken the country, and emotions rocketed from despair to wild enthusiasm and back again. Despite successes along the coasts and in the border states, northern efforts to secure a quick victory had failed. The South proved it could win on the battlefield, but a decisive victory eluded it. By the end of the year, both sides faced the grim reality of a long and tragic war.

TOP: The Stone (or Matthew) House, Manassas (Bull Run), VA, 1862. **MIDDLE:** The Stone Bridge across Bull Run, destroyed during the Union retreat, Manassas (Bull Run), VA, 1861. **BOTTOM:** Confederate General Thomas "Stonewall" Jackson.
PHOTOS COURTESY LIBRARY of CONGRESS

Casemate and Parrott Rifle, Fort Sumter, Charleston, SC.

PHOTO ©JAMES P. ROWAN

The first battleground of the Civil War was not a field with marching columns of soldiers but the stark walls of Fort Sumter, rising straight from the water's edge. Guarding Charleston Harbor, South Carolina, the fort became a symbol of national sovereignty when South Carolina seceded from the Union. It also became a testing ground for the new United States president.

Seven states left the Union after the election of Abraham Lincoln and formed the Confederate States of America. They seized federal property throughout the South and demanded the transfer of Fort Sumter into their hands. Lincoln refused and sent a ship to resupply the eighty-four-man garrison with food.

Before the fort could be strengthened, the southerners began a bombardment on April 12, 1861. Edmund Ruffin, an uncompromising seces-sionist, fired one of the war's first hostile shot, sending a shell crashing into the fort's walls. Ruffin would also fire one of the last shots of the conflict. Four years later, when his home lay in ruins and abandoned, he placed the muzzle of a gun in his mouth and pulled the trigger. On that day in 1861, Captain Abner Doubleday answered with a cannon shot from the besieged fort. An artillery duel continued through the day and into the next as the Confederate guns battered the thick walls. Doubleday described the scene of devastation as fire swept through the fort.

"The roaring and crackling of the flames," he wrote, "the dense masses of whirling smoke, the bursting of the enemy's shells, and our own which were exploding in the burning rooms, the crashing of the shot, and the sound of masonry falling in every direction, made the fort a pandemonium."

Major Robert Anderson, the Union commander, resisted the attack for thirty-four hours before ordering his men to surrender. As the defenders raised and again lowered the flag on April 14, the war claimed its first life. Ammunition exploded during an artillery salute, killing one Union soldier and mortally wounding another.

In 1863, the Union forces attempted to recapture Fort Sumter. Land batteries and a naval squadron bombarded the Confederates for days, pounding the five-foot-thick walls to rubble, but the soldiers refused to surrender. On April 14, 1865, four years to the day when Major Anderson had ordered the lowering of the United States flag, he returned to raise the same torn banner over the ruins of Fort Sumter.

Artillery and morning fog, Henry Hill, Manassas (Bull Run), VA.

PHOTO ©CHARLES GURCHE

Confederate general Thomas "Stonewall" Jackson rode slowly along the line of troops on Henry Hill as the First Battle of Manassas raged. His men were lying below the hillcrest, partially sheltered from an intense cannonade of exploding shells, as the Union army pressed its attack. "Steady men," Jackson told them, "all's well. All's well." But all was not well.

In the first major battle of the war, untested armies of half-trained soldiers faced each other. The Confederates, commanded by general Pierre G.T. Beauregard, had deployed behind Bull Run to protect the vital rail junction of Manassas and waited an attack. Here he was reinforced by General Joseph E. Johnston's troops. The surrounding countryside would become one of the most bitterly contested regions during the war, the scene of recurring clashes from major battles to partisan raids.

Before dawn on July 21, Union general Irwin McDowell had sent his forces around the left flank of his enemy, catching them off guard. Vastly outnumbered at first, the Confederates fought a delaying action that allowed troops arriving on Henry Hill to make a stand. After holding his forces back for two hours, Jackson sensed the moment had come and ordered his men forward. "Fire and give them the bayonet," he shouted, "and when you charge, yell like furies!"

The Confederates rushed forward, driving the Union soldiers from the hilltop. Exposed to an open field of fire, neither side could hold the position for long. After it changed hands repeatedly, southern reinforcements, which had arrived by train, tipped the scales. For the first time in United States history, railroads had changed the outcome of a battle. Soon the entire Confederate line pressed for-

ward in a final attack that swept the battlefield. When the retreating Union soldiers encountered a suspension bridge blocked by wreckage, panic took hold and the disorderly retreat turned into a rout.

Throughout the South, ecstatic crowds celebrated their first decisive victory, while despair in the North soon changed to renewed determination. Volunteers began flooding the recruiting stations. At the time, Manassas was the most costly battle in American history, with combined losses of almost 5,000 men. But the record did not last long. A year later, the armies would suffer more than 22,000 casualties when they met again on the same battlefield. At the Second Battle of Manassas, Confederates under General Robert E. Lee defeated the forces of Union general John Pope. This victory set the stage for Lee's invasion of Maryland, which would end with the battle of Antietam.

1862:
NOT WAR BUT MADNESS

It was a year of battles on a scale unimaginable only months before. During 1862 the fighting grew to epic proportions as tens of thousands of men collided at such places as Shiloh and Antietam. In Fredericksburg, 180,000 soldiers faced each other in the last month of the year, and many of them never left the battlefield.

I stopped there one winter, walking along the foot of Marye's Heights, where the Union dead once lay piled in windrows. Wave after wave of soldiers had charged into the converging fire of cannon and riflemen massed behind a stone wall on the hillside above, rising steeper than I had imagined. The kept grounds had a stillness to them, a vacuum left in the wake of a battle where more than 8,000 Union soldiers fell in utterly futile assaults. A reporter who witnessed the carnage put it bluntly. "It was not war," he wrote, "it was madness." Building in intensity, the conflict had become a cataclysmic force, and rational minds struggled to make sense of it.

The second year of war began with Union armies from the Potomac River to the trans–Mississippi preparing to launch attacks they hoped would crush the rebellion. As George McClellan readied his forces in Virginia, the North achieved early successes in the river war farther west. Gunboats pounded the Confederate defenders, and armies laid siege to forts guarding the strategic waterways.

On the Cumberland River in Tennessee, Union general Ulysses S. Grant captured Fort Donelson and its garrison of more than 12,000 soldiers. But Nathan Bedford Forrest slipped through the lines and escaped with a force of 700 men who would plague the North until hostilities ended. With the fall of Fort Donelson, Grant won the first major Union victory of the war, driving the Confederates from Kentucky and much of Tennessee. And then they caught him by surprise.

At dawn on April 6, a Confederate army commanded by Albert Sidney Johnston struck at the unsuspecting Federals near Shiloh Church. The first day of bitter fighting ended with the Union army being driven back and many taking shelter below the bluffs of the Tennessee River. Reinforced that night, Grant counterattacked the next morning to reverse the course of the battle and win a costly victory. The vast numbers of casualties from two days of savage fighting—nearly 24,000 men—shocked the country.

Along the Mississippi River, Union troops captured Island Number 10 while the battle still raged at Shiloh. Earlier, they had won a clear victory at Pea Ridge to keep their grip on the vital border state of Missouri. On April 24, Flag Officer David Farragut ran a gauntlet of Confederate batteries and destroyed the supporting fleets to capture New Orleans, the South's largest city. Memphis fell next. The Federals

TOP: Dunker Church and fatalities of Antietam, MD, 1862. **MIDDLE:** Union troops and captured Confederate cannon, The Peninsula, VA, 1862. **BOTTOM:** Union Major General Ulysses S. Grant.
PHOTOS COURTESY LIBRARY of CONGRESS

OPPOSITE: The New York Monument seen from inside the Maryland Monument, Antietam, MD. PHOTO ©LAURENCE PARENT

1.

2.

3.

4.

1: Confederate artillery near the Hornets' Nest, Shiloh, TN.
2: Machinery displayed at Tredegar Iron Works, Richmond, VA. **3:** Headstones of unknown Union soldiers in Antietam National Cemetery, Sharpsburg, MD. **4:** Detail of The Confederate Monument, Shiloh, TN.
OPPOSITE: Confederate artillery on Prospect Hill, Fredericksburg, VA.

TOP: Monitor, the *U.S.S. Onondaga*, on the James River, VA, 1860s. **MIDDLE:** The Army of The Potomac encamped at Cumberland Landing, VA, 1862. **BOTTOM:** Gunboat and unidentified monitor patrolling the James River, VA, 1864.
PHOTOS COURTESY LIBRARY of CONGRESS

were now close to clearing the Mississippi and cutting off the westernmost states of the Confederacy.

Having entered the war without a navy of its own, the South built a small fleet of armored ships. On March 8, one of the first Confederate ironclads attacked a Union fleet blockading Hampton Roads on the Virginia coast. The *Virginia* surprised the Northerners by quickly sinking two ships before returning to port. Next morning it resumed the hunt only to encounter a vessel unlike any seen before. The *Monitor*, an experimental Union ship built of iron plates, had arrived at night. Riding low in the water and topped by a revolving turret, one Confederate officer thought it resembled a floating cheese box. The two ships fought a duel for hours at point-blank range, but neither could strike a crippling blow. The *Virginia* returned to port and did not challenge the *Monitor* again, but the encounter that day transformed naval warfare. Wooden-hulled vessels suddenly became obsolete.

In the East, Richmond remained the goal of the northern leaders. Take it, they believed, and the Confederacy would crumble. During the spring, Union general McClellan transported the Army of the Potomac to Fort Monroe and Newport News, Virginia, where the soldiers slowly advanced up the peninsula. A small rebel force delayed him at Yorktown, buying enough time for the Confederates under Joseph Johnston to gather in defense of their capital. On May 31, Johnston attacked the invading army at Seven Pines and fell wounded. Robert E. Lee, who would quickly emerge as one of the great leaders of the war, took command.

In the Shenandoah Valley of Virginia, Confederate general Thomas "Stonewall" Jackson hit his northern enemies with lightning strikes and then suddenly disappeared. He outmaneuvered three pursuing armies, defeating each in turn, and left them stunned. His campaign prevented 60,000 Union troops from joining McClellan, and he eventually slipped away to unite with Lee's army outside Richmond. While Jackson stirred up the dust in the Shenandoah, J. E. B. Stuart led his cavalrymen in a bold raid, riding completely around the Army of the Potomac. The enemy's right flank, he discovered, lay unprotected. Seizing the opportunity, Lee struck McClellan on June 26 and began a week of desperate attacks known as the Seven Days Battles. Taking high casualties, he pushed the Union forces back to the protection of their gunboats on the James River, where they no longer posed an immediate threat to Richmond.

Having checked McClellan, Lee took the initiative and moved swiftly to attack the army of John Pope. After a stunning victory at Second Manassas, Lee continued advancing north and crossed into Maryland. McClellan, having resumed command, engaged the Confederates at Antietam Creek on September 17. With both sides suffering enormous losses, the Union army battered the Confederates but could not drive them from the battlefield. Between dawn and dusk, the opposing armies lost 22,700 men—dead, wounded, or missing.

Lee held his ground for another day, and when McClellan did not resume the attack he led his army back to Virginia. The impact of this withdrawal on the outcome of the war was tremendous. It gave Lincoln the opportunity to claim a victory and issue the preliminary Emancipation Proclamation, setting the stage for the eventual abolition of slavery. Farther west, Braxton Bragg launched a parallel invasion of the North, leading his army into Kentucky after General Edmund Kirby Smith had taken Lexington. But on October 8, Union forces blocked the Confederate advance at Perryville, and Bragg retreated after the battle.

Two decisions occurred at this time, both controversial and with implications to the present day. The Confederacy initiated the first draft in American military history, and the United States Congress enacted the nation's first income tax to pay for an increasingly costly war.

In mid-December, Lee won an overwhelming victory at Fredericksburg. In a prelude to the main Union attacks on Maryre's Heights, the South experienced the terror of urban warfare for the first time. The federal army under Ambrose Burnside bombarded the colonial city, shocking many southerners who felt the general had crossed an unspoken line. Shock turned to outrage when the Union soldiers sacked the town after a brutal street-by-street fight.

The second year of war ended with battles still raging. Confederate raiders under John Hunt Morgan struck deep into Kentucky, while an expedition under Bedford Forrest swept through western Tennessee. At Stones River in Tennessee, Union general William Rosecrans and Confederate general Braxton Bragg fought a pitched battle resulting in a slim victory for the North when the Confederates withdrew. But the South took heart with the repulse of an amphibious force under Union general William Tecumseh Sherman at Chickasaw Bayou, Mississippi.

The South had won major battles during the year but failed to secure either a decisive victory or recognition from the European powers. While opposed to slavery, Great Britain was sympathetic to the Confederacy since its mills were dependent on imported cotton. But it chose not to break the blockade. The North had retained control of the vital border states and gained strategic victories along the western rivers. But the chance of either side winning the conflict in a decisive battle grew slim. Facing the realities of a bitterly contested war, leaders in the North now believed victory would only come with the utter defeat of the South. Reconciliation based on compromise was no longer a viable option. By late December the war's end appeared far away, and both sides settled in for a fight to the finish.

At midnight on the last day of the year, church bells rang in Boston as the Emancipation Proclamation took effect, an event that changed the character of the war. The northern forces now became armies of liberation, fighting to preserve the Union and to end slavery. In a message to Congress, Lincoln reminded the country of what was at stake.

"Fellow citizens," he said, "we cannot escape history… The fiery trial through which we pass will light us down, in honor or dishonor, to the latest generation… In giving freedom to the slave, we assure freedom to the free—honorable alike in what we give and what we preserve. We shall nobly save, or meanly lose, the last best hope of earth."

TOP: The Rappahannock River and Fredericksburg, VA, 1860s. **MIDDLE:** Abraham Lincoln meeting with General George B. McClellan following the battle at Antietam, Maryland, 1862. **BOTTOM:** Confederate General Robert E. Lee, Commander of the Army of Northern Virginia.
PHOTOS COURTESY LIBRARY of CONGRESS

Early morning at Bloody Pond, near the Peach Orchard, Shiloh, TN.

PHOTO ©JEFF D. NICHOLAS

Cannon fire shattered the Sunday morning quiet on April 6, a time when the peach trees were in bloom. Suddenly thousands of Confederate soldiers poured out of the woods in a surprise attack on the Union army bivouacked near the Tennessee River. Henry Morton Stanley, who later gained fame as an explorer and journalist, charged forward with the Dixie Greys. The roar of battle surprised the young private. "Again and again," he recalled, "these loud and quick explosions were repeated, seemingly with increased violence, until they rose to the highest pitch of fury, and in unbroken continuity. All the world seemed involved in one tremendous ruin."

Earlier in the year, Grant had cleared the Confederates from much of Tennessee and moved to seize the vital rail junction at Corinth, Mississippi. But ordered to unite with another army, Grant held his soldiers at a steamboat stop called Pittsburg Landing and waited. With his attention focused on striking the enemy, the general let his guard down.

At dawn a Confederate force of 44,000 men led by general Albert Sidney Johnston swept into the outlying Union camps near Shiloh Church. Hit hard, the forward lines of Grant's 40,000-man army collapsed and many fled to the river. Others rallied in a sunken road, and for six hours a firestorm swirled around this new position with such ferocity it became known as the "Hornet's Nest."

The defenders repulsed a dozen Confederate attacks until late afternoon, when both wings of the Union line unraveled, leaving the middle nearly surrounded. Some soldiers fought their way out of the pocket, but 2,250 were captured. Their stubborn resistance had bought time, preventing the Confederates from pressing their attack. Many expected the shattered Union army to use the cover of darkness and escape across the river. Grant had other ideas.

Heavily reinforced during the night, he turned on his pursuers and attacked. The second day of battle seesawed back and forth until late afternoon, when the Confederates realized they could not win and retreated. At the end of battle the losses were tallied, and 24,000 soldiers—more than one in five who fought—were casualties.

The Union armies had driven a wedge deep into the South, and the victory at Shiloh secured their gains. But many blamed Grant for the carnage, and newspapers demanded his resignation. "I can't spare this man," Lincoln said; "he fights."

Union artillery at Malvern Hill Battlefield (Seven Days Battles), Richmond, VA.

PHOTO ©JEFF GNASS

The nerve center of the rebellion—Richmond, Virginia—stood defiantly close to Washington, DC. Only 100 miles separated the two warring capitals, and the North desperately wanted to capture it. When George McClellan was given command of the Army of the Potomac, he inherited the job of taking Richmond.

McClellan landed his army of 100,000 men at Fort Monroe and Newport News in March and early April of 1862 and turned inland toward the Confederate capital. Slowly, to the great aggravation of Lincoln, he marched his army up the peninsula. More than two months later, he reached the outskirts of Richmond and prepared to invest and bombard the city, only six miles away. Before he had his guns in place, the Confederates attacked.

The battle of Seven Pines on May 31 ended without a win for either side, but it left the southern leader, Joseph Johnston, seriously wounded. This loss became the Confederacy's gain when Robert E. Lee took command. On June 25, McClellan moved cautiously forward and triggered the first engagement in a week of fierce combat known as the Seven Days Battles. Lee, showing an audacity that surprised his friends and enemies, attacked the Union army the next day at Mechanicsville and kept attacking. Shaken by Lee's aggressiveness, and believing he was outnumbered, McClellan ordered a retreat to the James River. It became a running fight.

Lee attacked again at Gaines' Mill, at Savage's Station, at Frayser's Farm (Glendale), and finally at Malvern Hill, taking high casualties and losing all but one fight. He was willing to take these losses to drive the Union invaders away from the capital. And the losses were severe: 21,000 for the South and 16,000 for the North. By saving Richmond, Lee became a Confederate hero, and the North would not seriously threaten the Confederate capital again for two years.

By the end of May, 1864, Ulysses S. Grant had fought his way close to the old battleground of Gaines' Mill. A cavalry skirmish at Cold Harbor grew into a major engagement and a nightmare for the North. At dawn on June 3, Grant launched a headlong assault, sending 50,000 troops against Lee's dug-in troops. A Confederate officer called it "a contest to the death."

Of the thousands of Union soldiers lost that day, most fell in the first catastrophic minutes of the charge. It was not a contest but a slaughter. Taking defeat in stride, Grant continued to pressure Lee as the conflict entered a new phase of trench warfare.

Artillery and Dunker Church, Antietam, MD.

PHOTO ©PAT & CHUCK BLACKLEY

A Maryland woman watched them march past, looking as "lean and hungry as wolves." Crossing the Potomac River in early September, the Confederate soldiers were taking the war to the North for the first time. The stakes were high. Robert E. Lee needed a headline-grabbing win on northern soil to gain European recognition of the Confederacy.

George McClellan moved out of Washington, keeping the Union army between Lee and the nation's capital. When McClellan discovered Lee had divided his forces, he decided to attack. The Confederates fought a delaying action at South Mountain, as Lee urgently gathered his forces near the town of Sharpsburg. McClellan broke through the mountain gaps and prepared for battle along Antietam Creek.

At dawn on September 17, the Union army swung into Lee's left wing as artillery swept a corn-field held by the Confederates. It left a grim harvest. "The slain," recalled a Union general, "lay in rows precisely as they had stood in their ranks a few moments before." And that was only the beginning.

By mid-morning the field had changed hands a dozen times and left 8,000 men dead or wounded. The epicenter of the battle now shifted to a sunken farm road held by the Confederates. The Union attacks upon it came in swarms, and at one point achieved a breakthrough. But McClellan, unaware he outnumbered Lee two to one, feared a counterattack and held his reserves back. By the end of the fighting here, the bodies of hundreds of soldiers filled Bloody Lane in a "battalion of the dead."

McClellan's last chance rested with the 12,500-man force under the command of Ambrose Burnside now attacking the Confederate right wing. After three assaults, they finally drove back the 500 Confederates defending a bridge over Antietam Creek and pushed forward. At the moment of victory, reinforcements from Harper's Ferry rushed into the fray and blindsided the Union soldiers. Lee had narrowly escaped the destruction of his army, and at the end of the day still held his ground. After twelve hours of fighting, almost 23,000 of the 90,000 men engaged in the struggle had fallen or been captured. America has never matched that dark record for a single day of combat.

The next day was a stand-off until evening when the Confederates slipped across the Potomac. By forcing Lee to return to Virginia, the North won a strategic victory with enormous repercussions. Antietam gave Lincoln the position of strength he needed to announce the preliminary Emancipation Proclamation and reframe the war as a fight to end slavery.

OPPOSITE: Wildflowers bordering Antietam Creek at Lower (or Burnside) Bridge, Antietam, MD. PHOTO ©LAURENCE PARENT

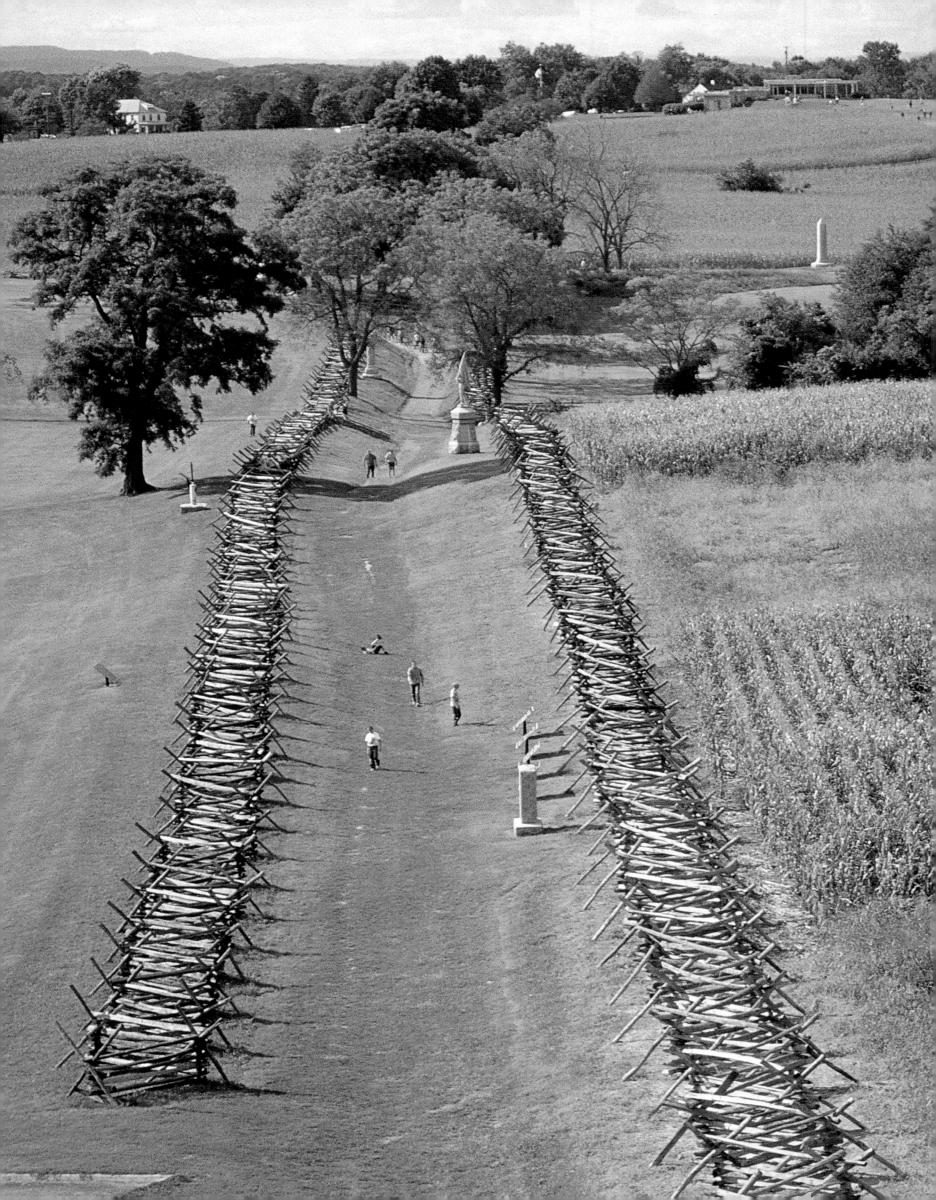

1.

PHOTO ©JEFF D. NICHOLAS

2.

PHOTO ©JEFF D. NICHOLAS

3.

PHOTO ©JEFF D. NICHOLAS

4.

PHOTO ©JEFF D. NICHOLAS

1: Marye's Heights, Fredericksburg, VA. **2:** Detail of The Confederate Monument, Shiloh, TN. **3:** Detail of Irish Brigade Monument at Sunken Road (Bloody Lane), Antietam, MD. **4:** Artillery at Hazel Grove, Chancellorsville Battlefield, Fredericksburg/Spotsylvania, VA.

OPPOSITE: Overview of Sunken Road (Bloody Lane) and surroundings, Antietam, MD.

PHOTO ©CHRIS E. HEISEY/PLACE STOCK PHOTO.COM

29

Union artillery at Chatham Manor, Fredericksburg, VA.

PHOTO ©JEFF GNASS

Even before the battle began, the new Union commander was in trouble. Ambrose Burnside's advance on Richmond had stalled at Fredericksburg, giving the Confederates time to strengthen their defenses. Burnside told his generals he planned to hit his opponents where they least expected it. He would surprise them, he said, by launching a frontal assault on their strongest point. The only ones surprised were his own generals.

At dawn on December 11, Confederate gunfire drove away the Union engineers trying to bridge the Rappahannock River. In response Burnside ordered his artillery to shell the town, hoping to dislodge the defenders. Jane Beale, one of the many civilians taking shelter in their homes, remembered the shrieking of shells and the crashing of solid shot through the upper stories of her house. "The agony and terror of the next hours," she wrote, "is burnt in on my memory as with a hot iron. I could not *pray* but only *cry* for mercy."

When the bombardment failed to end resistance, Union infantrymen filled pontoon boats and crossed the river in an amphibious assault. Hidden rifles crackled, and a rain of lead churned the waters around them as bullets whacked into the sides of the boats and sent splinters flying. Once across, the soldiers quickly established a beachhead and soon pushed the Confederates back from the waterfront, allowing the bridge to be completed.

As the battle raged in the streets of Fredericksburg, Clara Barton crossed the river to join the soldiers. The pontoon bridge swayed under her, "the water hissing with shot on each side," she recalled. Reaching the bank, a fragment of exploding shell ripped away part of her dress, and as she entered the burning town the soldiers cheered the woman who later founded the American Red Cross. Having fought a delaying action, the Confederates withdrew to their main line of defense on Marye's Heights, a half mile outside town.

Burnside spent the next day gathering his forces and began his attacks on December 13. One of his grand divisions breached Lee's right wing but was soon thrown back. The Union commander next ordered more than a dozen frontal assaults on Marye's Heights. Up to six ranks of Confederate riflemen, backed by massed cannons, defended their position by firing steady volleys from behind a stone wall. In a single day, 8,000 Union soldiers fell while charging the wall, and none ever reached it.

Fredericksburg was one of the worst Union disasters of the Civil War, but strategically the victory gained little for the South. To win the war

The Kirkland Monument near Marye's Heights and Sunken Road, Fredericksburg, VA.

PHOTO ©JAMES P. ROWAN

Lee had to do more than defeat the northern forces; he had to destroy them. And the following spring he came close.

Over the winter, Joseph Hooker replaced Burnside and brought the army back to fighting trim. In late April, he surprised the Confederates by swinging around their left flank. Lee quickly responded, leaving part of his army to guard Fredericksburg and sending the rest nine miles west to resist Hooker's advance at a crossroads known as Chancellorsville.

When the battle commenced on May 1, 1863, Lee's divided army faced an enemy that vastly outnumbered it. But as soon as the Confederates counterattacked, Hooker lost his nerve. He pulled back his troops, and from that point on Lee called the shots. Next day the Confederate commander took one of the greatest gambles of the war. He again divided his army in the face of the enemy and gave Stonewall Jackson 30,000 men to march twelve miles and launch a surprise attack on the Union right flank. With the remaining 14,000 troops, Lee had to create an illusion of strength to discourage an attack on his own thin lines.

Stonewall Jackson, in one of his most brilliant performances, hit the Union army with the force of an avalanche, and by dark had pushed it back more than two miles. Preparing to renew the attack, Jackson and his staff scouted beyond their lines at night and, as they returned, took fire from their own men. Hit three times, Jackson was carried from the field critically wounded and died a few days later.

On May 3, the Confederates continued the assault and took Hazel Grove. From this command-ing knoll, their artillery dominated the battlefield and drove back the Union forces from the cross-roads. Meanwhile, other Federals had stormed Maryre's Heights and now threatened Lee's rear. He again split his army and soon neutralized this danger. By the time he turned his attention back to Hooker's main force, the battle had ended and the northerners began recrossing the river.

Chancellorsville, Lee's greatest victory, came at a tremendous cost. The death of Jackson was an irreparable loss for the South. During the battle, Lee had asked his men to do the impossible and they had succeeded. He would ask them to do it again in the days ahead, as he turned north and prepared to invade Pennsylvania.

1863:
THE EPIC BATTLES

In the North, the year began with a sense of foreboding. Progress in the war had come slowly and at great cost. What victories they had gained were overshadowed by stunning losses. Even among northerners, Lincoln's proclamation to end slavery had proven to be politically divisive.

Union forces in the west began a second attempt to take Vicksburg, and more than two months passed without success. In Virginia, Joseph Hooker took command of the Army of the Potomac, still camped across the river from Fredericksburg. After reorganizing the army and infusing the demoralized troops with new hope, he led them into another debacle. At Chancellorsville, in early May, the fighting spirit of the Confederate soldiers matched the audacity of their two finest generals, Robert E. Lee and Stonewall Jackson. The spectacular win convinced Lee the time had come to force a decisive battle. Seven weeks later, he marched the Army of Northern Virginia into Pennsylvania on a second invasion of the North.

The Army of the Potomac followed, keeping between Lee and Washington, DC. Under a new commander, George Meade, it closed with the Confederates at the town of Gettysburg on July 1. A wounded officer, falling into Confederate hands, was surprised by the kind treatment he received. "I could not but feel," wrote Alfred Lee, "that they were after all not only my fellow-men, but fellow-countrymen, and wonder how it is that merely artificial differences of opinion could ever array us as deadly enemies to each other."

By the end of the first day of fighting, the southerners had the upper hand, and the next day saw them nearly succeed in breaking the Union lines. For the soldiers facing each other at Gettysburg on July 3, the fate of a nation seemed to hang in the balance. The pivotal moment of the battle had come as the Confederate army prepared its final attack.

To walk the ground those soldiers crossed that day, I asked historian Ed Bearss to lead me along the route of Pickett's Charge. We stood on Seminary Ridge, where the Confederate formations had gathered, and I listened as he brought the past alive. "Men of old Virginia," he said, repeating the words of Major General George Pickett, "prepare to charge the enemy!"

More than 12,000 Confederate soldiers marched in perfect order that afternoon with their bayonets flashing in the sun. Watching from Cemetery Ridge, a mile away, the Union soldiers saw the Confederates rapidly advancing. An officer compared the charge to a force of nature, describing the scene as "an overwhelming, resistless tide." And he waited for it to sweep over them.

TOP: Dead Confederate sharpshooter, Devil's Den, Gettysburg, PA, 1863. **MIDDLE:** The Army of The Potomac encamped at Belle Plain, Virginia, prior to the Battle of Chancellorsville in 1863. **BOTTOM:** Confederate soldiers taken prisoner during the battles at Gettysburg, PA, 1863.
PHOTOS COURTESY LIBRARY of CONGRESS

OPPOSITE: Mississippi Memorial on Seminary Ridge, sunrise, Gettysburg, Pennsylvania. PHOTO ©CHRIS E. HEISEY/PLACE STOCK PHOTO.COM

TOP: Dead Confederate soldiers following the battles at Gettysburg, PA, 1863. **MIDDLE:** Bomb-proof shelters of Logan's troops below the Shirley House, Vicksburg, MS, 1863. **BOTTOM:** Lookout Mountain, Chattanooga, TN.
PHOTOS COURTESY LIBRARY of CONGRESS

After crossing a mile of open ground, Bearss and I stopped next to a cannon marking the Union lines. "Alonzo Cushing," he said, "has had two of his guns pushed up here. He's had them double-charged with canister. He's been shot in the fleshy part of the leg, shot in the groin, shot in the fleshy part of each of the arms, and he gives the command, 'Fire!' and as he pulls the lanyard a bullet goes in his mouth."

At that moment, the Virginians surged over a stone wall in front of the cannons. "They are vaporized," he said. "Meanwhile, other Confederates are coming on fast; they're crowding up; it's a mob; they've lost all order whatsoever."

In the chaos, soldiers on each side fought fiercely, thrusting bayonets and firing at point-blank range. "We were crazy with the excitement of the fight," remembered Lieutenant William Harmon of the 1st Minnesota. "We rushed in like wild beasts. Men swore and cursed and struggled and fought, grappled in hand-to-hand fight, threw stones, clubbed their muskets, yelled and hurrahed!"

Only a few hundred Confederates made it across the wall, and their momentum quickly faltered in the face of stiff resistance. "In five minutes," Bearss said, "it's all over." Cheers swept the Union lines as the most colossal battle ever fought in North America came to an end. In two months, Lee had gone from his greatest victory to his worst defeat.

To the west, Ulysses Grant's star was rising. In April, he crossed the Mississippi River below Vicksburg. For three weeks, Grant skillfully maneuvered his forces and eventually encircled the city, which Abraham Lincoln believed was the key to winning the war. The Union army laid siege to Vicksburg on May 25, and 40 days later its garrison of 30,000 soldiers surrendered. On July 4, the day Lee began his retreat back to Virginia, the Stars and Stripes flew over the main southern stronghold on the Mississippi River.

Having gained control of the Mississippi, the North had split the Confederacy in two. The dual victories of Gettysburg and Vicksburg in the summer of 1863 appeared to seal the fate of the Confederacy.

John Hunt Morgan provided a flicker of hope for the South during an otherwise disastrous July. His cavalrymen swept through Kentucky, Indiana, and Ohio in a daring raid covering 700 miles. The Confederate troopers spread fear through those states until Morgan was captured with what remained of his force late in the month.

That summer, African-American regiments got their first taste of combat and a chance to prove their bravery under fire. They surprised many northern skeptics by their courage at Port Hudson on May 27, again at Milliken's Bend on the Mississippi on June 7, and the next month at Fort Wagner, South Carolina. In that action the 54th Massachusetts spearheaded a frontal assault on a heavily fortified position, losing half of its men. By the end of the war, nearly 179,000 black soldiers would serve in the Union army.

In Tennessee, William Rosecrans maneuvered Braxton Bragg into evacuating Chattanooga, a crucial rail junction on the Tennessee River. Then Bragg, reinforced by 15,000 men from Lee's Army of Northern Virginia, turned the tables. During the chaotic fighting at Chickamauga on September 18–20, the Confederates won a complete victory and drove the Union army back to Chattanooga. A desperate rearguard action by George Thomas, one of the North's finest commanders, saved the army from destruction.

Lieutenant Keller Anderson, a Confederate with the 5th Kentucky, barely survived the murderous gunfire received during their assault on Thomas' position. "Thud!" he wrote, "and down goes Private Robertson. He turned, smiled, and died. Thud! Corporal Gray shot through the neck. 'Get to the rear!' said I. Thud! Thud! Thud! Wolf, Michael, and the gallant Thompson. Thud! Thud! Thud! Courageous Oxley, the knightly Desha, and duty-loving Cummings. And thus it goes. The fallen increase and are to be counted by the hundreds."

Suddenly, the impact of a bullet spun Anderson to the ground where he lay wounded, listening to the rebel yell rising over the battlefield. He recalled how his hair stood on end whenever he heard "that penetrating, rasping, shrieking, blood-curdling noise that could be heard for miles on earth, and whose volume reached the heavens—such an expression as never yet came from the throats of sane men."

Following the Union defeat, Lincoln placed Grant in charge of all armies from the Appalachian Mountains to the Mississippi. Under his leadership, the Federals soon broke the siege of Chattanooga and prepared to go on the offensive. Drawing on units stationed in Virginia, the North transported 20,000 reinforcements by rail in a matter of days. Grant's combined forces now hit the enemy hard.

Between November 23 and 25, the Union army attacked the strong Confederate defenses on Lookout Mountain and Missionary Ridge. Grant had called for an attack on the north end of Missionary Ridge, supported by a diversion on the center which was thought to be impregnable. Instead, the most successful frontal assault of the war happened spontaneously when the soldiers, without orders, turned the diversionary action into a full-scale charge up the mountainside. The Union soldiers drove the defenders from their entrenched positions and won a decisive victory. When a Confederate attempt to retake Knoxville failed a few days later, the bitter contest for East Tennessee ended.

In Virginia, Lee and Meade continued to spar with each other but neither general landed a decisive blow. Lee's attempt to slip between the Army of the Potomac and Washington ended in failure, and Meade's efforts to turn Lee's flank in the Mine Run campaign sputtered to a halt.

The North won major victories in 1863, which changed the course of the war, but they came at a price. The loss of men on the battlefield and the expiration of enlistments depleted the Union ranks, forcing Lincoln to initiate the first federal draft. Riots broke out in New York City and, as mobs rampaged for three days, soldiers marched straight from the battlefield at Gettysburg to restore order. The South faced even greater troubles. In many clashes, the Confederate army lost a higher percentage of its strength than the Federals, and its losses were becoming increasingly difficult to replace.

In a single year, the fortunes of the North had undergone a stunning reversal. By the end of 1863, Lincoln was confident of ultimate victory and began planning for the post-war restoration of the Union. The South appeared to be on the ropes, but its tenacity in the face of defeat would match that of the Union troops in their darkest days. The conflict was far from over. More men would die in the fighting after Gettysburg than before.

TOP: Union General George Gordon Meade, Commander of The Army of The Potomac during the battles at Gettysburg, PA. **MIDDLE:** The Mississippi River's busy wharves at Vicksburg, TN, 1863. **BOTTOM:** Union General George Thomas—the "Rock of Chickamauga."
PHOTOS COURTESY LIBRARY of CONGRESS

1.

2.

3.

4.

1: Detail of Ohio infantry monument, Vicksburg, MS.
2: Cemetery Ridge near the site of Pickett's Charge,
Gettysburg, PA. **3:** Cavalry statue featured on the
Wisconsin Memorial, Vicksburg, MS. **4:** Selfridge Battery
and Naval Memorial, Vicksburg, MS.
OPPOSITE: Confederate artillery and the Virginia
Memorial, Seminary Ridge, Gettysburg, PA.

Cemetery Ridge monuments and artillery at the monument dedicated to the High Water Mark of The Confederacy, Gettysburg, PA.

PHOTO ©LAURENCE PARENT

After the battle of Gettysburg, local resident Tillie Pierce climbed a rocky outcrop to view the carnage. "From the summit of Little Round Top," she later wrote, "surrounded by the wrecks of battle, we gazed upon the valley of death beneath. The view there spread out before us was terrible to contemplate! It was an awful spectacle! Dead soldiers, bloated horses, shattered cannon and caissons, thousands of small arms. In fact, everything belonging to army equipments was there in one confused and indescribable mass."

More than 158,000 soldiers had clashed at Gettysburg during three days in July. It was the largest battle ever fought in America, and the bloodiest. What Tillie Pierce saw was only one corner of a battlefield where 51,000 men were lost in the fighting.

The campaign had begun in early June. The Army of Northern Virginia was on the move and did not stop until it reached the Union heartland. An invasion made sense to Confederate general Robert E. Lee, who needed to resupply his army from the prosperous farmlands in the North. Lee also wanted to preempt another federal drive against Richmond and relieve pressure on the Confederate forces in the western theater. Most importantly, he needed to force the Union army into a decisive confrontation. He could not afford to merely win battles; he had to destroy his enemy's will to fight.

When Lee entered Pennsylvania, both sides knew they were on the verge of a momentous battle. On July 1, a sharp engagement between leading elements of the southern army and Union cavalry on the outskirts of Gettysburg quickly flared. The sound of battle drew forces into the vortex from all points of the compass, and Confederate reinforcements pressed the attack until the Union lines broke.

Late in the day, federal soldiers fled through town to the high ground on Cemetery Hill, where they took a stand. That night both armies grew in strength, as arriving regiments filled the Union lines and the Confederate positions a mile west on Seminary Ridge. The next day, 75,000 men in southern gray faced more than 90,000 in northern blue. The Union soldiers not only had an advantage in numbers, but occupied the strongest position. George Meade, the new Union commander, decided to keep the Army of the Potomac in place and wait for an attack.

Statue of Union Brigadier General G.K. Warren, Little Round Top, Gettysburg, PA.

PHOTO ©DIANNE DIETRICH-LEIS

Lee was more than willing to oblige. On July 2, he ordered an early morning advance against the Union left wing, but corps commander James Longstreet delayed until the afternoon. When his men finally went into action, they aggressively charged an exposed position in advance of the main Union forces. Intense fighting raged as the North came close to losing the battle.

General G. K. Warren, inspecting the Union lines, discovered they had not posted soldiers on Little Round Top, the key to their defenses. He ordered the nearest troops to occupy it. As they raced to the crest, Confederates were sweeping up the far side. The fighting grew savage, and the day was saved by the 20th Maine, and other Union regiments, courageously holding their ground. Longstreet also came close to breaking the Union lines on Cemetery Ridge farther north. Only a counterattack by the 1st Minnesota, which lost 68 percent of its regiment in 15 minutes, bought enough time for reinforcements to arrive.

The crux of the battle came the next day, July 3rd. That morning, Confederates who were threatening Meade's right wing were driven off Culp's Hill. Then a midday lull in the fighting was suddenly broken by a massive Confederate barrage directed against Cemetery Ridge. After two hours, the firing stopped and Pickett's Charge began.

Lee, a master at surprising his enemy, did exactly what Meade anticipated this time. The Confederates, with Pickett's division in the lead, swept across the fields of Gettysburg and hit the Union center on Cemetery Ridge. They grappled in a wild, chaotic struggle until most Confederates were lying dead, wounded, or ready to surrender. Other remnants broke to the rear and dodged back to their lines on Seminary Ridge. The battle ended with the South losing more than a third of its army.

Late the next day, the Army of Northern Virginia began its long retreat. It had lost the battle, but the bravery and sacrifice of its soldiers allowed them to honorably accept the defeat, a rehearsal for the surrender at Appomattox Court House nearly two years later. A few months after the battle, Abraham Lincoln stood among the Union graves on ground where soldiers had literally been torn apart in the fighting. The country had a deep need to make sense of the continuing slaughter, and in his moving Gettysburg Address Lincoln affirmed the nobility of those who had given their last full measure for the cause of freedom.

Union artillery, Illinois Memorial, and Shirley House seen from the 3rd Louisiana Redan, Vicksburg, MS.

PHOTO ©JEFF GNASS

By the beginning of 1863, the Confederacy had come close to losing control of the Mississippi River. It was the job of Ulysses Grant to clear the last 200-mile stretch between Port Hudson and Vicksburg.

His forces spent the winter months probing without success for weaknesses in the Confederate defenses. By late April, Grant had marched his army below the heavily fortified city of Vicksburg and had begun ferrying his troops across the Mississippi. The next three weeks saw his soldiers win five battles against two Confederate armies and place a stranglehold on Vicksburg, defended by troops under general John Pemberton.

After mounting two failed attacks, Grant settled in for a long siege, hoping to either starve or hammer the Confederates into submission. He bombarded the city with 220 cannon and used boat-mounted mortars to throw 218-pound shells into the citadel. The Confederates had dug in, building a network of forts, redoubts, and entrenchments to withstand the daily barrages. And many of the city's residents took refuge in underground shelters.

"My heart stood still," wrote a woman under siege, "as we would hear the reports from the guns and the rushing and fearful sound of the shell as it came toward us. As it neared, the noise became more deafening; the air was full of the rushing sound; my ears were bursting. And as it exploded, the report flashed through my head like an electric shock, leaving me in a quiet state of terror."

Union engineers trenched to within yards of the enemy lines, and twice they exploded mines beneath the Confederates. By late June, Grant had built his army to 77,000 men who faced 30,000 defenders weakened by the attrition of combat, disease, and scant rations. They were reduced to eating pea bread, supplemented by horse, mule, and occasional rat meat.

On July 4, the 40th day of the siege, Pemberton surrendered to Grant. Although facing starvation, many of the Rebel soldiers felt betrayed by their leaders. They smashed their guns and shredded their battle flags rather than have them captured. When Port Hudson lowered the Confederate flag a few days later, the entire Mississippi River lay in Union hands, severing the states of Texas, much of Louisiana, and Arkansas from the Confederacy. Grant's reputation as a fighting general skyrocketed, and Lincoln eventually placed him in command of all Union armies.

"The fate of the Confederacy was sealed," Grant later wrote, "when Vicksburg fell."

Split-rail fence and Brotherton Cabin, Chickamauga Battlefield, GA.

PHOTO ©PAT & CHUCK BLACKLEY

A spectacular Confederate victory at Chickamauga in the fall of 1863 was matched by an equally stunning defeat two months later. Both battles were fought for control of Chattanooga, a crucial rail center on the Tennessee River. By holding it, the Union army could disrupt Confederate supply lines and use it as a base to invade Georgia.

After the Confederates under Braxton Bragg abandoned the city, Union commander William Rosecrans thought he had them on the run. On September 18, they turned on their pursuers at Chickamauga Creek and attacked. The next day, massive charges hammered the Union lines, again and again, until night brought an end to a day of savage fighting.

Bragg renewed his assault on the 20th. After numerous repulses, the Confederates found a gap in the enemy lines and poured through. Many of the Union troops, including Rosecrans, streamed back to the defenses of Chattanooga. "Disorganized masses of men were hurrying to the rear," recalled a southern general; "batteries of artillery were inextricably mixed with trains of wagons; disorder and confusion pervaded the broken ranks struggling to get on."

George Thomas, a southerner who had remained loyal to the United States, gathered the remnants of the Union army and formed a new line. Mounting an epic stand, he prevented the Confederates from destroying the fleeing army. Two days of fighting at Chickamauga resulted in 34,500 casualties, the bloodiest battle in the western theater.

For two months, Bragg laid siege to Chattanooga until a dramatic night operation opened the way for food to reach the hungry federal army. Pontoon boats filled with troops floated silently past Confederate pickets, enabling the Union soldiers to seize a bridgehead at Brown's Ferry. The Union army, now under the overall command of Ulysses Grant, took the offensive.

On November 24, the Federals stormed the Confederate stronghold on Lookout Mountain, and next day the action shifted to Missionary Ridge. The initial assault stalled, and as a diversion, soldiers in the center were ordered to take the entrenchments at the foot of the mountain. After swiftly overrunning these, they found themselves exposed to intense fire from above. Without orders, they continued charging up the mountainside.

"The colors rushed in advance," remembered a Union general, "and the men crowded toward the banners. Each regiment became a wedge-shaped mass, the flags at the cutting edge cleaving the way to the summit." Against all odds, the attack succeeded in driving the Confederates off the ridgetop. By nightfall, the Union forces had defeated a major southern army and opened the way to Atlanta.

1.

2.

3.

4.

1: Union artillery on Little Round Top, sunset, Gettysburg, PA. **2:** Artillery relief on the Wisconsin Memorial, Vicksburg, MS. **3:** Chattanooga seen from atop Lookout Mountain, TN. **4:** Artillery at Craven House, Chattanooga, TN. **OPPOSITE:** Dogwood and headstones in Vicksburg National Cemetery, MS. PHOTO ©DICK DIETRICH

1864:
SCORCHED EARTH

The great struggle, already the most destructive conflict in American history, took a more savage turn in the third year of the war. It went from open battles to trench warfare, and from episodic clashes to fighting so sustained one battle merged with the next. It became total war, where armies left behind them a countryside in smoking ruins.

Battlefields commemorate the past, but only a few evoke it as powerfully as Spotsylvania. On the recommendation of park historian John Hennessy, I traveled to Bloody Angle, a scene of fighting so ferocious some survivors could not bear to record it. Fierce combat had marked the war at every turn but never on such a scale or for such a prolonged period.

A path followed the edge of the woods where the Confederate army had placed its lines in a wide curve along the high ground. They stacked logs chest high and banked them with earth dug from trenches. Over time the earthworks had eroded into a rounded berm, leaving only a hint of the buried past. The landscape itself had changed little. An open field rolled down to thick woods closer to the Confederate position than I had imagined. The battleground seemed too confined for the tens of thousands who converged here on May 12, 1864.

On that morning, Union infantry in ranks forty men deep attacked across the open ground, hidden by drifts of fog. They overran the Confederate defenses until driven back to the outer face of the earthworks. For twenty hours, they battered each other in the most ruthless hand-to-hand combat of the war. One witness recalled how a "frenzy seemed to possess the yelling, demonic hordes on either side."

Soldiers fired point-blank through chinks in the parapet walls, swung their muskets as clubs, slashed with swords, and pinned each other to the ground with bayonets. A volume of fire never before experienced killed and maimed men by the thousands and pounded flat the bodies left exposed. Bullets whittled away at the trunk of a tall oak, twenty-two inches thick, until it fell crashing onto the defenders during the night. Rain continued to pour down and the gullies ran blood red as the dying were trampled into the mud underfoot. The fighting did not end when the dead lay four deep nor did it end at dark. It only subsided when the battle fury had run its course, long after dark.

TOP: Gathering the remains of those killed at Cold Harbor, Richmond, VA, 1865. **MIDDLE:** Skeletal remains and cannon-blasted forest following The Battle of The Wilderness, Fredericksburg/Spotsylvania, VA. **BOTTOM:** Graves of Union soldiers at City Point, Petersburg, VA. PHOTOS COURTESY LIBRARY of CONGRESS

Standing here at Bloody Angle, I felt uneasy. After the battle, a Union general counted 150 bodies jumbled together in a space measuring roughly 12 feet by 15 feet. The terrifying intensity of those hours had fused with the landscape, making it difficult to separate one from the other. I took off walking across the open field to put

OPPOSITE: Ellwood (Lacy House), Headquarters of the Union's 5th Corps during The Wilderness Campaign, Fredericksburg/Spotsylvania, VA. PHOTO ©CHARLES GURCHE

TOP: Columbiad gun at Fort Darling (Drewry's Bluff) overlooking the James River below Richmond, VA. **MIDDLE:** Union Major General William Tecumseh Sherman. **BOTTOM:** Sherman's Union troops destroying rail lines in Atlanta, GA, 1864.
PHOTOS COURTESY LIBRARY of CONGRESS

some distance between myself and that dark ridgeline.

Bloody Angle marked a year when the war itself had taken on a more brutal character. In Georgia, Tecumseh Sherman's march to the sea left in its wake a 60-mile-wide path of burning farms, twisted rails, and slaughtered livestock. Union armies carried out other scorched-earth operations in the Shenandoah Valley and the northern Piedmont of Virginia. In retaliation, Confederate raiders in Pennsylvania burnt the center of Chambersburg, and agents attempted to do the same in New York City.

In early March, Confederates had ambushed a detachment of Union cavalrymen who were attempting to penetrate the defenses of Richmond and free prisoners of war suffering under terrible conditions. They captured about a hundred of the raiders and killed their young colonel, Ulric Dahlgren. Papers found on his body outraged the South and opened a mystery still unresolved. The documents recorded Dahlgren's secret plans to burn the city and assassinate Confederate president Jefferson Davis and members of his cabinet. Northern officials denounced the papers as forgeries, but historians have made a strong case for their authenticity. The incident further inflamed southern animosity toward the invaders.

In late winter, Abraham Lincoln appointed his fighting general, Ulysses Grant, as the supreme commander of all Union armies. Grant's strategy was simply to destroy his enemy not capture territory. "When in doubt," he said, "fight."

President Lincoln sent an expeditionary force up the Red River in mid–March, but after two months it had failed to gain its objective: the capture of Shreveport, Louisiana. The situation in Georgia was more encouraging. Sherman had marched his army out of Chattanooga in early May and forced the Confederate army to fall back toward Atlanta.

On the eastern front, Grant now faced the legendary Army of Northern Virginia for the first time. The Union army crossed the Rapidan River to open its spring offensive and began traversing the Wilderness, a region containing parts of the Chancellorsville battlefield. Lee, using the thickly wooded terrain to offset his numerical disadvantage, sent his troops forward to make contact. On May 5, the battle erupted.

Lee was able to block the Union advance in a chaotic two-day fight, but gained little advantage when Grant did not retreat the way other Union commanders had done before. Despite heavy losses, Grant pressed on. He shifted his forces past the Confederate flank and angled closer to Richmond. Lee matched him move for move and again checked the northern army at Spotsylvania Court House. Another desperate battle lasted ten days, leaving Lee with a tactical win but without having ended the threat to the Confederate capital. The day after the battle at the Bloody Angle, a messenger informed Lee of the death of the great cavalry commander J. E. B. Stuart, mortally wounded in a fight at Yellow Tavern.

Grant, the most tenacious general Lee had faced, continued to bypass the Confederates. And then, ten miles from Richmond, he ran head-on into Lee's forces at Cold Harbor. On June 3, the Union army attacked the entrenched Confederates and lost 5,000 men, most of them falling in sixty terrifying minutes. Grant's worst defeat gave Lee his last great victory.

The active phase of Grant's Overland Campaign, lasting two months, had cost the North 55,000 casualties, nearly half of its combat strength. The Confederate losses numbered 27,000 men, but these were soldiers who could not be replaced. Grant understood the ruthless calculus of war. The Union army could continue taking twice as many casualties as the Confederates and still win. Time was working against the Confederacy. Undeterred by Cold Harbor, Grant kept pushing. He crossed the James River and shifted his army toward Petersburg, a rail center vital to the survival of Richmond.

Direct assaults by the Union army at Petersburg failed to dislodge the defenders, and by mid-summer they were resigned to a war of attrition. Lee had little choice but to keep his soldiers in the trenches. To relieve pressure on his front, he sent Confederate general Jubal Early on a lunge into Maryland from the Shenandoah Valley. The Confederates won a fight at Monocacy on July 9, and reached the outer defenses of Washington before turning back to Virginia. Grant, unrattled, held his ground outside Petersburg. That fall Union general Philip Sheridan eliminated the threat from Early by winning a series of victories and forcing the Confederates to abandon much of the Shenandoah.

Anti-war sentiment had been growing in the North as the bloodletting grew worse. Lincoln saw his prospects for being reelected in the fall begin to fade. And then Sherman delivered a major victory. In Georgia, the Union forces pushed the Confederates back to within striking distance of Atlanta. Fierce battles on the outskirts forced the defenders, now under John Bell Hood, to abandon the city. On September 2, Sherman's triumphant army entered Atlanta, and two months later Lincoln won a solid victory in the presidential election.

Atlanta was only the beginning. Severing ties to his supply base, Sherman led a mobile force of 60,000 men on a march to the sea. He began a sweep through the heartland of the South designed to break the will of the people to resist. "I can make the march," said Sherman, "and make Georgia howl!"

Soldiers were ordered to destroy anything of military value, and then they burned and pillaged everything in their path. Leaving behind a belt of devastation, Sherman linked up with the federal fleet and occupied Savannah on December 21. He was still not finished. He turned his army north and prepared to roll through the Carolinas.

Meanwhile, Hood's Confederates launched a counterstrike into Middle Tennessee to isolate Sherman. They hit the Federals with repeated punches and, after the battle of Franklin, forced them to withdraw to Nashville and join forces with George Thomas. The tough Union commander struck back with overwhelming force and crushed Hood on December 15, all but destroying the southern army.

In summing up the year, Confederate officer John Esten Cooke wrote, "From 1861 to 1864 the war was war. Thenceforth it was slaughter." Lee now commanded the only substantial military force in the Confederacy. But for many southerners, unwilling to admit defeat, that was enough. As long as the Army of Northern Virginia survived destruction, they believed the South had a fighting chance.

TOP: Breastworks of Confederate Fort Mahone, Petersburg, VA, 1865. **MIDDLE:** Union General Philip Sheridan. **BOTTOM:** Union breastworks at Fort Sedgwick used during the seige of Petersburg, VA, 1865.
PHOTOS COURTESY LIBRARY of CONGRESS

Monuments at Bloody Angle, Spotsylvania Battlefield, VA.

PHOTO ©PAT & CHUCK BLACKLEY

Ulysses S. Grant took command of all Union armies in the late winter of 1864 and went on the attack. The victor of Fort Donaldson, Vicksburg, and Chattanooga attached himself to George Meade's Army of the Potomac. Heading a force of 118,000 men, he set out to crush the 61,000 troops of the Army of Northern Virginia, commanded Robert E. Lee. His strategy was to draw Lee into open battle by threatening Richmond.

On May 5, the Confederates collided with Grant's army in the Wilderness, opening the first engagement of the Overland Campaign. For two days they fought in terrain choked by tangled woods, and in the ferocity of the battle bullets stripped off the bark, turning the trees white. Fires ignited by muzzle flashes swept through the undergrowth, burning alive the wounded left on the field. As the battle veered back and forth, Grant's coolness under fire steadied the other Union leaders. When the momentum reversed and the Confederates faced defeat, Lee's leadership and the eleventh-hour arrival of reinforcements saved the day for the South. Grant lost 18,000 men, but no matter what the cost he was determined not to back off.

Finding himself blocked, Grant side-stepped the Confederates and angled southeast. Lee anticipated the move and, after a night march, intercepted Grant at the crossroads of Spotsylvania Court House. Fierce attacks over a ten-day period failed to break Lee's lines. A bulge in the Confederate defenses became the epicenter of the battle, with its most intensely contested sector known as Bloody Angle. Union forces had temporary success here on May 10, encouraging Grant to try again with a massive assault.

Two days later, 20,000 troops captured the most exposed Confederate entrenchments. Lee, determined to retake the position, threw in all available forces. In close combat, they gained most of what they had lost and fought viciously to keep it. Bullets filled the air. "Some sounded like wounded men crying," a southerner recalled; "some like the humming of bees; some like cats in the depth of the night, while others cut through the air with only a 'Zip' like noise."

Before dawn, the Confederates slipped away to a new defensive line, and the fighting eased. After periodic flare-ups, the battle drew to a close a week later. By mid-summer both sides had dug in at Petersburg, south of Richmond, where they faced months of trench warfare.

Reconstructed Union earthworks and artillery at Battery 9, Petersburg, VA.

PHOTO ©JAMES P. ROWAN

Five railways converged on Petersburg, twenty–three miles south of the Confederate capital. Ulysses S. Grant knew if he could capture this transportation hub, Richmond would fall. Pulling his forces out of the Cold Harbor lines, he slipped away without alerting Robert E. Lee to his plans.

On June 15, advance units of the Union army attacked the lightly manned defenses of Petersburg but failed to exploit their initial success. The Confederates held out long enough for Lee's army to arrive and establish new defenses. Facing a long siege, both armies began constructing a vast complex of trenches, redoubts, and bomb-proof shelters. Eventually the entrenchments extended for thirty-seven miles, stretching Lee's manpower to the limit.

As weeks grew into months, the opposing armies kept shelling and sniping at each other with periodic attempts by Grant to break the enemy de-fenses. The most spectacular attack occurred at the Crater on July 30. A regiment of Pennsylvania coal miners dug a tunnel 510 feet long and packed four tons of gunpowder beneath a Confederate stronghold. They detonated the charge at dawn, opening a 170-foot-long breach in the lines that obliterated most of two Confederate regiments and a six-gun battery.

"A great fountain of red earth rose to a great height," wrote a Union soldier, "mingled with men and guns, timbers and planks, and every·kind of debris, all ascending, spreading, whirling, scattering and falling with great concussion to the earth once more."

The follow-up assault collapsed into a chaotic struggle as the Confederates recovered from the initial shock and counterattacked. Shells exploded among the Union soldiers crowded in the crater, and riflemen poured down fire from the rim turning it into a death trap. The battle ended with the North having suffered nearly 4,000 casualties.

Grant absorbed these losses and continued to press Lee. His forces cut a major rail line on August 18, reducing the Confederates to near starvation rations. Desertions further weakened Lee's army during the grim winter months, and by spring he knew they had to abandon Petersburg. To open an escape route, Lee ordered a desperate attack on Fort Stedman on March 25, 1865. His forces, too weak to exploit an initial breakthrough, were forced to pull back with heavy losses. Grant now realized the end was near.

The supreme commander of the Union army threw his men forward in a general assault on April 2. The Confederates resisted until dark, when the last soldier left the trenches that Lee's army had held for nearly ten months. The longest siege in American history had come to an end.

Confederate artillery on Kennesaw Mountain, GA.

PHOTO ©JEFF D. NICHOLAS

Union soldiers advanced deep into northern Georgia in the spring of 1864, led by William Tecumseh Sherman. He intended to capture the strategic rail center of Atlanta, and crush Joseph Johnston's Confederate army. After weeks of fighting and maneuvering, Sherman launched a direct assault against fortified lines on Kennesaw Mountain.

A furious shelling opened the battle on June 27, followed by the attack. Clawing through tangled undergrowth, the Union infantrymen charged into blasts of canister and heavy gunfire from riflemen concealed behind earthworks. Thousands of soldiers soon became locked in fierce combat across the mountainside. And, suddenly, a stillness settled over a pocket of the battlefield.

Confederate officer William Martin ordered his men to cease firing as flames swept rapidly in front of his lines, burning alive some of the Union casualties. "Come and remove your wounded," he shouted; "they are burning to death. We won't fire a gun until you get them away." Soldiers who had been killing each other moments before, both Union and Confederate, rushed between the lines to rescue the wounded and carry them to safety.

Sherman ordered his men to fall back when the assault stalled, but they did not retreat. In the following days, a series of flanking movements and sharp engagements brought the Union army to the outskirts of Atlanta. Worried Confederate leaders replaced Johnston with John Bell Hood, a more aggressive commander, as Sherman bombarded the city. The Union general disregarded civilian casualties in his determination to inflict maximum damage, igniting outrage in the southern press.

After several weeks, the Union soldiers pulled out of their trenches and turned south. They surprised the Confederates by destroying the last open railway at Jonesboro. With his lifeline cut, Hood was forced to evacuate Atlanta on September 2. Fleeing soldiers torched eighty railcars of ammunition to keep them from falling into enemy hands.

"The flames shot up to a tremendous height," wrote a resident, "and the exploding missiles scattered their red hot fragments right and left. The very earth trembled as if in the throes of a mighty earthquake." The next day Union troops marched into the city. "The long agony is over," an officer noted, "and Atlanta is ours!"

The fall of Atlanta reverberated through the North. Two months later, voters elected Abraham Lincoln to a second term, giving him a mandate to continue the war.

OPPOSITE: Flowering dogwood and artillery, Chickamauga Battlefield, GA. PHOTO ©LARRY ULRICH

1865:
AN AWED STILLNESS

Winter found the Army of Northern Virginia holding a maze of entrenchments outside Petersburg and Richmond. Under bombardment and half-starved, most soldiers placed their trust in Robert E. Lee, the general who had led them so far. Others lost hope. At night, men deserted by the score, returning to homes left unprotected and families growing hungry. Over the stark winter months, Lee watched his army fade away.

In the northern states, the press expressed frustration with the war's sluggish pace. They could not understand how the entire Confederate army, fielding only 100,000 men, could hold out against a combined Union force of almost a million soldiers. The campaign of Ulysses S. Grant to batter the South into submission, costing the lives of many thousands of men, had stalled in the trenches outside Petersburg. The shovel had replaced the rifle as the chief weapon of war.

Farther south, on February 1, Tecumseh Sherman actively began his march into South Carolina seeking victory and vengeance. His army engineered their way north through swamplands and across flooded rivers, throwing up bridges and laying down roads. Crossing into South Carolina, the columns of Union soldiers tore a path of devastation across the state that had triggered the rebellion. Sherman's men burned and pillaged as they drove toward the state capital, spreading fear among the civilian population.

On February 17, the Union army captured Columbia and fires engulfed the city. Sherman continued his march into North Carolina, facing only weak resistance from forces under Joseph Johnston. Fort Fisher, a coastal stronghold, had fallen earlier in the year, leading to the capture of Wilmington, the Confederacy's last Atlantic seaport. Union cavalry now raided through Alabama, North Carolina, and Georgia, destroying what remained of the Confederate military industry.

In the midst of a grim war, Abraham Lincoln's second inaugural address surprised many by its tone of reconciliation. On March 4, he stood on the steps of the Capitol. "With malice toward none," he said; "with charity for all; with firmness in the right, as God gives us to see the right, let us strive on to finish the work we are in; to bind up the nation's wounds; to care for him who shall have borne the battle, and for his widow and his orphan—to do all which may achieve and cherish a just, and lasting peace, among ourselves, and with all nations."

By early spring, Lee knew his army had no choice but to abandon Petersburg and attempt to join Johnston in North Carolina. On April 2, Grant launched an all-out assault and, with his only remaining supply line about to be cut, Lee ordered a

TOP: Ruins in Savannah, Georgia, following Sherman's "March to the Sea", 1865. **MIDDLE:** The "Dictator", a mortar used during the siege of Petersburg, VA, 1864. **BOTTOM:** Union rifles stacked outside of town after the fall of Petersburg, VA, 1865.
PHOTOS COURTESY LIBRARY of CONGRESS

OPPOSITE: The Courthouse in the village of Appomattox Court House, VA. PHOTO ©JEFF D. NICHOLAS

TOP: Canal Basin and the Burnt District, Richmond, VA, 1865. **MIDDLE:** Union General Ulysses S. Grant at Cold Harbor, VA. **BOTTOM:** Jefferson Davis, President of the Confederate States of America.
PHOTOS COURTESY LIBRARY of CONGRESS

retreat. His men held the inner defenses until night, buying enough time for the army to escape.

Word reached Richmond, and the Confederate leaders began to evacuate. Jefferson Davis caught the last train to leave the city, and the government was now on the run. Fire and chaos spread. After being under siege for ten months, the capital fell the following day, and the end of the Confederacy was at hand. On April 4, Lincoln walked the streets of Richmond, followed by a throng of liberated blacks, as fires still guttered and smoke hung in the air. A Union general had asked Lincoln for his advice on handling the defeated southerners. "If I were in your place," he said, "I'd let 'em up easy, let 'em up easy."

Confederate forces regrouped to the west at Amelia Court House only to find their provisions had not arrived. Lee let his men forage in the countryside, and Grant caught up. Burning bridges behind them, the Confederates retreated and the following days merged together in a nightmarish succession of rear-guard actions, night marches, and savage fights. Grant did not let up. The infantry kept pushing Lee west, while the cavalry raced ahead to capture supplies and block his escape.

Late on April 8, the exhausted Confederates reached Appomattox Court House and found themselves outnumbered five to one and about to be surrounded. Some officers argued for disbanding the army to carry on a guerilla war, a move encouraged by Jefferson Davis. Lee firmly opposed this option, realizing it would only prolong the suffering and engender a legacy of hatred.

Next day, the Confederate commander rode into the crossroads village to surrender, knowing he might be imprisoned. He entered the home of Wilmer McLean and began negotiating terms with Grant. Lee was surprised by the generosity of the Union general, who put into practice the desire for reconciliation expressed by Lincoln. The formal surrender took place three days later, when the Army of Northern Virginia infantry stacked arms for the last time. For an entire day, thousands of Confederates marched between rows of blue coated soldiers lining the road. Recognizing the courage of men who had fought against all odds, the Union troops honored them with a salute. No sound broke the silence as the soldiers marched past in what a Union officer called "an awed stillness . . . as if it were the passing of the dead."

The war ended at Appomattox, but the surrender stretched out for two and a half more months as the remaining forces laid down their arms or simply disbanded. Many Confederates, still willing to fight, had difficulty believing it was over. When a cavalryman heard the news from Appomattox, he stood up in his stirrups and lifted a clenched fist high above his head. "If General Lee has had to surrender his army," he shouted, "there is not a just God in Heaven."

On the evening of April 14, John Wilkes Booth slipped into the presidential box at Ford's Theater in Washington and shot Lincoln in the head with a single bullet. They carried the dying president across the street to the Petersen boarding house and into a cramped backroom. On that spring night, the wild joy of having won the war collapsed into despair. Bells tolled and anger seethed through the streets. Inside the Petersen house, confusion gripped the generals and cabinet officers who had gathered, unsure if another attack might be coming. The world had descended deeper into madness than they thought possible. Lincoln's death the next morning left the country adrift at the moment of victory.

On the high seas, the Confederate cruiser *C.S.S. Shenandoah* continued to fly the colors long after Appomattox. That June, the ship destroyed the New England whaling fleet in arctic waters, bringing its total captures to thirty-eight vessels. The *Shenandoah* then sailed south, and off the coast of California commanding officer James Waddell received confirmation of the war's end. But a deep sense of duty compelled him to finish his mission and not surrender. On November 6, the ship without a country reached England and lowered the Confederate flag for the last time, six months after the war had ended.

The American Civil War was fought primarily in the countryside. It was a war of cornfields, sunken roads, and peach orchards. By the time it ended, hundreds of thousands had lost their lives and numberless graves filled the battlefields and hometown cemeteries. People desperately needed to find meaning in those losses, and before his death Lincoln had assured them the sacrifice was not in vain. War had prevented the nation from fragmenting, but he kept reminding them of something more. What gave the war a higher purpose was the freeing of four million slaves, an act that restored the nation's revolutionary claim of liberty and equality for all.

At Appomattox Court House, I expected to find a place set aside to commemorate a last stand in a lost cause. Maybe it was the dogwoods in bloom that day, but as I approached the McLean House I kept walking. In a field down the road, I found where the common soldiers had surrendered their weapons and with great sorrow, bringing tears to the eyes of even their enemy, gave up their battle-torn flags. Of all places, this site should have evoked a sense of loss. Instead, men who had been fighting three days before faced each other for the last time in mutual respect, and then went home. Lee put it this way, "It is our duty to live."

It was springtime when the war ended, which may be why Lee's thoughts had turned to planting when they worked out the terms of surrender. The general asked Grant if his men could keep their horses. In the Confederate army, he explained, the soldiers supplied their own horses, and they would need them to put in a crop when they returned to their homes. Grant, who had once struggled as a farmer and failed, readily agreed. It was a simple act that let the defeated soldiers place their trust in the future instead of the past.

On my way to Appomattox, I had seen two old men putting in a garden with what had been a horse-drawn plow hitched to a pickup. One guided the plow and the other steered the truck. It was springtime in Virginia and time to plant. And it was a time of hope. A message on a highway sign nearby read, "Appomattox County, Where Our Nation Reunited."

TOP: The capitol of the Confederate States, Richmond, VA, 1865. **MIDDLE:** Commander of the Confederate Army of Northern Virginia, Robert E. Lee. **BOTTOM:** President Abraham Lincoln four days before his assassination in April, 1865. PHOTOS COURTESY LIBRARY of CONGRESS

The McLean House, site of Robert E. Lee's surrender to Ulysses S. Grant, Appomattox Court House, VA.

PHOTO ©JEFF GNASS

They had been on the run since abandoning the defenses of Petersburg, pressed hard by the pursuing Union forces. On April 8, the Confederates lost the race to Appomattox Station, where supply trains waited for them. Phil Sheridan's cavalry had swept ahead and seized their food and, with enemy on all sides, the Army of Northern Virginia was trapped. Not knowing the strength of Sheridan's force, its only chance was to attempt a breakthrough. Robert E. Lee, knowing the Confederacy would collapse if he surrendered, ordered an attack the next morning.

At dawn on April 9, the Confederate soldiers formed their battleline for the last time. Gaunt with hunger, they stepped out with military precision and charged the enemy. The Union troops dropped back, uncovering an overwhelming force of blue coated soldiers ready to fight.

Lee had lost the gamble and called off the assault. He now had no choice but to meet with Ulysses S. Grant.

That afternoon the Confederate general sat in the parlor of a house owned by Wilmer McLean, a refugee from northern Virginia. McLean's home near Manassas had been Confederate headquarters early in the first battle of the war and a cannon shell had crashed through his kitchen roof. As the ebb and flow of armies ravaged his lands, he sold up and moved to the quiet backwater of Appomattox to wait out the war, hoping to never see another soldier.

The commander-in-chief of the Union armies arrived late, mud-splattered and wearing a private's coat. Lee sat across from him in a dress uniform ready to negotiate the terms of surrender. After working out certain practicalities, Grant

added an important provision that prevented federal authorities from disturbing the Confederates as long as they remained peaceful and obeyed the law. This established a policy of reconciliation rather than retribution.

After Lee signed, Grant introduced him to his staff. Shaking hands with Ely Parker, a Seneca Indian, Lee studied his features.

"I am glad to see one real American here," he said.

"We are all Americans," Parker answered in words distilling the tragedy of the war.

On April 12, the day the Confederates laid down their arms, slaves on a nearby plantation gathered in front of the main house to hear their master speak. "Men and women," he announced, "you are as free as the birds that fly in the air."

OPPOSITE: Artillery at Hazel Grove, Chancellorsville, Fredericksburg/Spotsylvania, VA. PHOTO ©CHARLES GURCHE

1. PHOTO ©JEFF GNASS

2. PHOTO ©JEFF D. NICHOLAS

3. PHOTO ©JAMES P. ROWAN

4. PHOTO ©TERRY DONNELLY

1: National Cemetery at Andersonville N.H.S., Georgia.
2: Arkansas River at Arkansas Post N. Mem., Arkansas.
3: Artillery and memorial at Brices Cross Roads N.B.S., Mississippi. **4:** Split-rail fence and fog-shrouded forest on Pinnacle Peak, Cumberland Gap N.H.P., Kentucky.

ANDERSONVILLE NATIONAL HISTORIC SITE
ANDERSONVILLE, GEORGIA.

Officially known as Camp Sumter, Andersonville was built in 1864 to accommodate the large number of Union prisoners sent from Richmond. The site continued in operation for 14 months and gained national notoriety as the largest of the Civil War prisons. It housed more than 45,000 prisoners, nearly 13,000 of whom died from sickness, malnutrition, or exposure. After the war, the government declared the ground where these soldiers were buried a national cemetery. This cemetery, along with the prison grounds, makes up the 495 acres that today constitute the Andersonville National Historic Site. Upon its establishment in 1970, Congress declared that the park was intended to serve as a memorial to both the Union prisoners who lost their lives at Andersonville and to American prisoners of war from all conflicts. The hope was to honor the imprisoned soldiers who died here and to further an understanding of these camps and their place in the nation's history.

ARKANSAS POST NATIONAL MEMORIAL
GILLETT, ARKANSAS.

Located fifty river miles up the Arkansas River from its convergence with the Mississippi, Arkansas Post occupied an important strategic position. Operating from the newly constructed Fort Hindman, the Confederates launched gunboat assaults on Union vessels, threatening shipping on the Mississippi. By late 1862, the northern pressure to secure the river had reached a threshold. On January 9, 1863, in a prelude to the Vicksburg campaign, Union general John McClernand began an offensive against Arkansas Post. Federal troops landed downstream from the fort and attacked by land, while armored gunboats fired from the river. The fighting continued for two days until the afternoon of January 11, when the Confederates surrendered Fort Hindman, reduced to ruins by the bombardment. Although the victory did little to help the campaign against Vicksburg, it removed an obstacle from the shipping lanes on the Mississippi and gave control of the mouths of the White and Arkansas Rivers to the Union.

BRICES CROSS ROADS NATIONAL BATTLEFIELD SITE
TUPELO, MISSISSIPPI.

Brices Cross Roads National Battlefield Site commemorates an encounter between Union Brigadier General Samuel D. Sturgis and Major General Nathan Bedford Forrest. The battle was intended to distract the Confederates from attacking the Nashville & Chattanooga Railroad—Major General William Sherman's supply line for more than 100,000 troops participating in the Atlanta campaign. On June 10, 1864, the two armies met at the crossroads. Although outnumbered more than three to one, the Confederates held their ground. Forrest eventually gained the advantage and drove Sturgis's troops into retreat. Not satisfied with a mere victory, however, Forrest pursued the fleeing Federals the next day, taking many prisoners and capturing much-needed supplies. The brilliant tactics employed by Forrest during this battle cemented his reputation as one of the best generals of the war.

CUMBERLAND GAP NATIONAL HISTORICAL PARK
MIDDLESBORO, KENTUCKY.

Cumberland Gap is located at the junction of three states: Virginia, Tennessee, and Kentucky. Formed by a break in the Appalachian Mountains, it opens a strategic passage between eastern and western states. The gap changed hands four times during the war without involving a major conflict. Fortified in 1861 by the Confederates and then abandoned, the site was unoccupied until Union General George W. Morgan arrived. He further strengthened the position in anticipation of a Confederate assault. The rebels, however, bypassed the gap and cut the Union supply line from behind, forcing Morgan to abandon the site. In September, 1863, a handful of Federals regained control of the gap by tricking the Confederates into believing they were a large army. The Union retained possession of the gap until the war's end.

FORT DONELSON
NATIONAL BATTLEFIELD
DOVER, TENNESSEE.

Fort Donelson was the site of the South's first major defeat of the war, costing them control of much of Tennessee and most of Kentucky. In February of 1862, knowing that Union forces were on their way, the Confederates reinforced their position and waited, convinced they outnumbered their opponents. Union Brigadier General Ulysses S. Grant took full advantage of this complacency and encircled the fort. The rebels, realizing their mistake, launched an all-out attack to break through the enemy lines. They were unsuccessful, and knowing defeat was imminent, the top brass fled by water under the cover of night with 2,000 soldiers. Colonel Nathan Bedford Forrest escaped overland with 700 of his cavalrymen. The remaining troops had no choice but to surrender. Grant captured more than 12,000 prisoners, along with weapons and supplies desperately needed by the South. This victory garnered Grant a promotion to major general while dealing a disastrous blow to the Confederacy.

FORT PICKENS
(GULF ISLANDS NAT'L SEASHORE)
GULF BREEZE, FLORIDA.

The largest of the forts protecting Pensacola Harbor, Fort Pickens was built just off the mainland on Santa Rosa Island. From this position, troops were able to simultaneously guard the harbor entrance and the island itself. This was of great tactical advantage and gave the Union an upper hand in several battles. Union Lieutenant Adam J. Slemmer realized the defensive opportunity Fort Pickens provided and relocated his entire command to the fort in January 1861. He based his decision on the fact that an enemy party had attempted to seize his previous post, the less-defensible Fort Barrancas. Some historians consider the shots fired during the encounter that drove Slemmer to Fort Pickens to be the opening shots of the Civil War.

FORT PULASKI
NATIONAL MONUMENT
SAVANNAH, GEORGIA.

Brigadier General Thomas W. Sherman landed his Union forces on Tybee Island in the winter of 1861. He planned to attack Confederate-controlled Fort Pulaski on neighboring Cockspur Island. Acting on the advice of his engineering officer, Sherman ordered his rifled cannons moved to the northwestern tip of the island, within range of the enemy fortification. Although the walls of Fort Pulaski were almost eight feet thick, the rifled cannons stripped away nearly half the thickness of the outer wall in the first day. By the next afternoon, the rebels had no choice but to surrender. Despite the incredible bombardment, only two men were killed in the battle—one Union soldier and one Confederate. In addition to preserving the fort itself, Fort Pulaski National Monument also protects the diverse array of plant and animal life found on Cockspur Island.

MONOCACY
NATIONAL BATTLEFIELD
FREDERICK, MARYLAND.

Monocacy is known as the battle that saved Washington, D.C. While not a large-scale encounter, it played a significant role in the defense of the northern capital. Throughout the summer of 1864, agents employed by Baltimore & Ohio Railroad president John Garrett tracked the movement of Lieutenant General Jubal Early's army as it headed north. Recognizing the danger, Garrett notified the government of the Confederate advance, but little action was taken. Finally, he contacted Major General Lew Wallace directly. Acting on his own accord, Wallace gathered as many Union troops as he could find and stationed them at Monocacy Junction in anticipation of an attack. That attack came on the morning of July 9. Although heavily outnumbered, the Union soldiers held their ground for almost a day. This action delayed the Confederate advance and allowed reinforcements time to reach Washington. If Wallace had not intercepted Early at Monocacy, it is likely the next battle would have been fought for the capital itself.

1.   PHOTO ©JEFF GNASS

2.   PHOTO ©JAMES RANDKLEV

3.   PHOTO ©JAMES P. ROWAN

4.   PHOTO ©JEFF D. NICHOLAS

1: Artillery overlooking the Cumberland River, Fort Donelson N.B., Tennessee. **2:** Fort Pickens (Gulf Islands N.S.), Florida. **3:** Blasted wall at Fort Pulaski N.M., Georgia. **4:** Pond and the historic Gambrill Mill that now houses the Visitor Center, Monocacy N.B., Maryland.

1.

PHOTO ©CHRIS E. HEISEY/PLACE STOCK PHOTO.COM

2.

PHOTO ©JEFF D. NICHOLAS

3.

PHOTO ©JEFF D. NICHOLAS

4.

PHOTO ©JEFF GNASS

1: Pennsylvania Cavalry Monument, Oak Ridge, Gettysburg, PA. **2:** Detail of a bronze memorial plaque, Chickamauga Battlefield, GA. **3:** Union artillery near Taylor Farm, Petersburg, VA. **4:** The Watt House at Gaines' Mill, Richmond, VA.

OPPOSITE: Statue of Confederate General Thomas "Stonewall" Jackson on Henry Hill, sunset, Manassas, VA. PHOTO ©CHARLES GURCHE

1.   PHOTO ©JEFF D. NICHOLAS

2.   PHOTO ©JEFF D. NICHOLAS

3.   PHOTO ©JEFF D. NICHOLAS

4.   PHOTO ©CHARLES GURCHE

1: Artillery and Elkhorn Tavern, Pea Ridge N.M.P., Arkansas. **2:** Shattered cannons at Stones River N.B., Tennessee. **3:** Artillery and memorial at Tupelo N.B., Mississippi. **4:** The Ray House, Wilson's Creek N.B., Missouri.

PEA RIDGE
NATIONAL MILITARY PARK
PEA RIDGE, ARKANSAS.

In March 1862, in an attempt to recover southwest Missouri, Major General Earl Van Dorn led 16,000 Confederate troops against the Union army at Pea Ridge. The fighting was split between Leestown and Elkhorn Tavern, two separate sites where troops under the command of Brigadier General Samuel Curtis intercepted the converging rebel divisions. Although outnumbered, the Federals routed the Confederates by the second day. Both sides suffered casualties, with Curtis losing 1,400 men and Van Dorn about 1,000. The South's defeat ended any serious threat to Missouri, and eventually led to the occupation by the Union of Arkansas north of the Arkansas River. The Pea Ridge National Military Park commemorates the conflict, preserving some 4,300 acres of the battlefield, including reconstructed Elkhorn Tavern, where some of the battle's heaviest fighting occurred. It also protects a two-and-a-half-mile remnant of the Trail of Tears, followed by eastern Indians on their forced removal to Oklahoma.

STONES RIVER
NATIONAL BATTLEFIELD
MURFREESBORO, TENNESSEE.

Stones River was one of the bloodiest battles of the Civil War and ended as a limited victory for the Union. The fighting took place between December 31, 1862, and January 2, 1863, with General William S. Rosecrans's Union army suffering an estimated 13,000 casualties—some 3,000 more than the Confederates. After the battle, General Braxton Bragg withdrew the southern army, surrendering control of Middle Tennessee. This loss of territory, coupled with a significant loss of life, dealt a serious blow to the rebels. General Rosecrans gained a needed victory for the North and won praise from President Lincoln. Along with the battlefield, the national park includes the Hazen Brigade Monument, thought to be one of the oldest Civil War memorials, and the Stones River National Cemetery, where some 6,000 Union soldiers are buried.

TUPELO
NATIONAL BATTLEFIELD
TUPELO, MISSISSIPPI.

In the summer of 1864, Major General William Sherman realized that Confederate Major General Nathan Bedford Forrest could threaten the success of his Atlanta campaign. The Union general ordered all measures be taken to detain Forrest in Mississippi. To this end, 14,000 Union troops under the command of Major General Andrew J. Smith advanced on Tupelo. The ensuing engagement lasted two days and cost the Confederates more than 1,300 men. Smith retreated but gained a strategic victory. He had been able to destroy portions of the Confederates' crucial Mobile & Ohio Railroad, and moreover, he had kept Forrest far away from Sherman's supply lines. The Tupelo National Battlefield, located within the Tupelo city limits, preserves a small part of this conflict.

WILSON'S CREEK
NATIONAL BATTLEFIELD
REPUBLIC, MISSOURI.

Wilson's Creek was the first significant Civil War battle to be fought west of the Mississippi River. As Missouri provided access to three major rivers, the state was of strategic importance. On August 10, 1861, the army of Confederate Brigadier General Ben McCulloch clashed with Union forces under Brigadier General Nathaniel Lyon. More than 10,000 Confederate troops engaged the smaller Union army of 5,400, claiming a quick and decisive victory. The Confederates, however, were unable to follow up their win, and most of Missouri remained under federal control for the rest of the war. During the fighting, Nathaniel Lyon was struck by a musket ball and became the first Union general to die during combat. The site remains almost unchanged, allowing visitors a rare opportunity to experience the battlefield as it appeared during the war.

RESOURCES & INFORMATION

ANDERSONVILLE NATIONAL HISTORIC SITE
496 Cemetery Road
Andersonville, GA 31711
(229) 924-0343
www.nps.gov/ande

ANTIETAM NATIONAL BATTLEFIELD
PO Box 158
Sharpsburg, MD 21782
(301) 432-5124 (Info), 432-7648
(HQ), www.nps.gov/anti

APPOMATTOX COURT HOUSE NATIONAL HISTORICAL PARK
Hwy 24, PO Box 218
Appomattox, VA 24522
(434) 352-8987x26
www.nps.gov/apco

ARKANSAS POST NATIONAL MEMORIAL
1741 Old Post Road
Gillett, AR 72055
(870) 548-2207
www.nps.gov/arpo

BRICES CROSS ROADS NATIONAL BATTLEFIELD SITE
2680 Natchez Trace Parkway
Tupelo, MS 38804
(800) 305-7417
www.nps.gov/brcr

CHICKAMAUGA & CHATTANOOGA NATIONAL MILITARY PARK
PO Box 2128
Fort Oglethorpe, GA 30742
(706) 866-9241
www.nps.gov/chch

CUMBERLAND GAP NATIONAL HISTORICAL PARK
US 25E, PO Box 1848
Middlesboro, KY 40965
(606) 248-2817
www.nps.gov/cuga

FORT DONELSON NATIONAL BATTLEFIELD
PO Box 434
Dover, TN 37058
(931) 232-5706
www.nps.gov/fodo

FORT PICKENS (GULF ISLANDS NATIONAL SEASHORE)
1801 Gulf Breeze Parkway
Gulf Breeze, FL 32563
(850) 934-2600 —or—
3500 Park Road
Ocean Springs, MS 39564
(228) 875-9057
www.nps.gov/guis

FORT PULASKI NATIONAL MONUMENT
Hwy 80 East, PO Box 30757
Savannah, GA 31410
(912) 786-5787
www.nps.gov/fopu

FORT SUMTER NATIONAL MONUMENT
1214 Middle Street
Sullivan's Island, SC 29482
(843) 883-3123
www.nps.gov/fosu

FREDERICKSBURG & SPOTSYLVANIA NATIONAL MILITARY PARK
120 Chatham Lane
Fredericksburg, VA 22405
(540) 371-0802, 373-6122
www.nps.gov/frsp

GETTYSBURG NATIONAL MILITARY PARK
97 Taneytown Road

Gettysburg, PA 17325
(717) 334-1124
www.nps.gov/gett

HARPERS FERRY NATIONAL HISTORICAL PARK
PO Box 65
Harpers Ferry, WV 25425
(304) 535-6298
www.nps.gov/hafe

KENNESAW MOUNTAIN NATIONAL BATTLEFIELD PARK
900 Kennesaw Mountain Drive
Kennesaw, GA 30152
(770) 427-4686
www.nps.gov/kemo

MANASSAS NATIONAL BATTLEFIELD PARK
12521 Lee Highway
Manassas, VA 20109
(703) 361-1339
www.nps.gov/mana

MONOCACY NATIONAL BATTLEFIELD
4801 Urbana Pike
Frederick, MD 21704
(301) 662-3515
www.nps.gov/mono

PEA RIDGE NATIONAL MILITARY PARK
PO Box 700
Pea Ridge, AR 72751
(479) 451-8122
www.nps.gov/peri

PECOS NATIONAL HISTORICAL PARK
PO Box 418
Pecos, NM 87552
(505) 757-6414
www.nps.gov/peco

PETERSBURG NATIONAL BATTLEFIELD
1539 Hickory Hill Road
Petersburg, VA 23803
(804) 732-3531
www.nps.gov/pete

RICHMOND NATIONAL BATTLEFIELD PARK
3215 East Broad Street
Richmond, VA 23223
(804) 226-1981
www.nps.gov/rich

SHILOH NATIONAL MILITARY PARK
1055 Pittsburg Landing Road
Shiloh, TN 38376
(731) 689-5696
www.nps.gov/shil

STONES RIVER NATIONAL BATTLEFIELD
3501 Old Nashville Highway
Murfreesboro, TN 37129
(615) 893-9501
www.nps.gov/stri

TUPELO NATIONAL BATTLEFIELD
c/o Natchez Trace Parkway
2680 Natchez Trace Parkway
Tupelo, MS 38804
(800) 305-7417
www.nps.gov/tupe

VICKSBURG NATIONAL MILITARY PARK
3201 Clay Street
Vicksburg, MS 39183
(601) 636-0583
www.nps.gov/vick

WILSON'S CREEK NATIONAL BATTLEFIELD
6424 West Farm Road 182
Republic, MO 65738
(417) 732-2662
www.nps.gov/wicr

ABOVE: Infantry statue featured on the Wisconsin Memorial, Vicksburg, MS. PHOTO ©JEFF D. NICHOLAS

63

ACKNOWLEDGMENTS

The publisher would like to extend his thanks to all those National Park Service employees wh o shared ideas, information, and enthusiasm with us during the production of this publication. Warmest thanks to Ed Bearss, Robert Casey, Ji m Jolly, Bill Price, David Wagner, Larry Swanson, Danica Buehren, Don Todd, and Shanna Hossley for reviewing the book while in proof-stage and special words of gratitude to Patty Loughin of Eastern National for her persistence in bringing this production to fruition. Thank You All! —JDN

PRODUCTION CREDITS

Publisher: Jeff D. Nicholas
Author: Scott Thybony
Editor: Nicky Leach
Battlefield Map by Darlece Cleveland
Printing Coordination: Sung In Printing America

SIERRA PRESS

4988 Gold Leaf Drive, Mariposa, CA 95338
(209) 966-5071, 966-5073 (Fax)

BACK COVER
Artillery at sunrise, Antietam, MD.
PHOTO ©LAURENCE PARENT
BACK COVER (INSET)
The Pennsylvania Memorial, Cemetery Ridge, Gettysburg, PA.
PHOTO ©CHRIS E. HEISEY/PLACE STOCK PHOTO.COM
BELOW
The Virginia Memorial at sunrise, Seminary Ridge, Gettysburg, PA. PHOTO© JEFF D. NICHOLAS

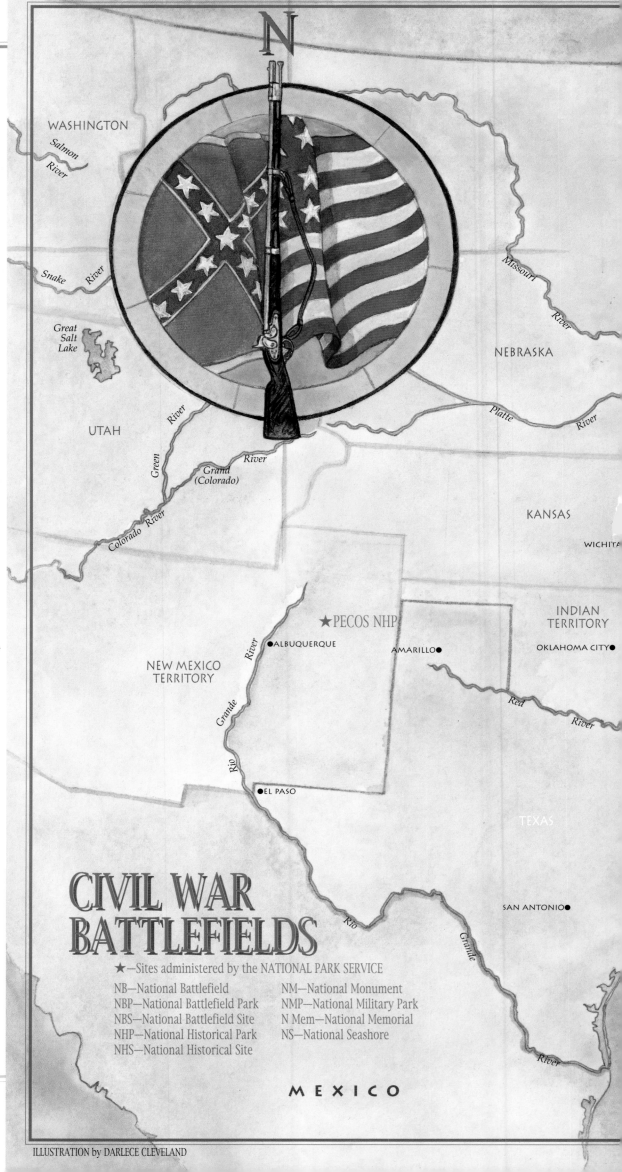

CIVIL WAR BATTLEFIELDS

★—Sites administered by the NATIONAL PARK SERVICE

NB—National Battlefield
NBP—National Battlefield Park
NBS—National Battlefield Site
NHP—National Historical Park
NHS—National Historical Site

NM—National Monument
NMP—National Military Park
N Mem—National Memorial
NS—National Seashore

ILLUSTRATION by DARLECE CLEVELAND